Disorderly Conduct

Books by Bruce Jackson

Folklore and Society (editor, 1966)

The Negro and His Folklore in Nineteenth-Century Periodicals (editor, 1967)

A Thief's Primer (1969)

"Wake Up Dead Man": Afro-American Worksongs from Texas Prisons (1972)

In the Life: Versions of the Criminal Experience (1972)

"Get Your Ass in the Water and Swim Like Me": Narrative Poetry from Black Oral Tradition (1974)

Killing Time: Life in the Arkansas Penitentiary (1977)

The Programmer (1979)

Death Row (with Diane Christian, 1980)

Get the Money and Shoot: The DRI Guide to Funding Documentary Films (1981; rev. ed. with Diane Christian, 1986)

Your Father's Not Coming Home Any More (editor, 1981)

Doing Drugs (with Michael Jackson, 1983)

Teaching Folklore (editor, 1984)

Law and Disorder: Criminal Justice in America (1985)

Rainbow Freeware (1986)

Feminism and Folklore (editor, 1987)

Fieldwork (1987)

A User's Guide: Freeware, Shareware, and Public Domain Software (1988)

The Centennial Index: 100 Years of the Journal of American Folklore (coeditor, 1988)

Disorderly Conduct (1992)

Disorderly Conduct

BRUCE JACKSON

Foreword by William M. Kunstler

University of Illinois Press
Urbana and Chicago

Manufactured in the United States of America
C 5 4 3 2 1

This book is printed on acid-free paper.

Library of Congress Cataloging-in Publication Data

Jackson, Bruce.
Disorderly conduct / Bruce Jackson ; foreword by William M. Kunstler.
p. cm.
Includes bibliographical references.
ISBN 0-252-01905-9 (alk. paper)
1. United States—Social conditions—1960–1980. 2. United States—Social conditions—1980– . 3. Crime—United States. 4. Vietnamese Conflict, 1961–1975—Protest movements—United States. 5. Drug abuse—United States. I. Title.
HN59.J33 1992
306'.0973'0904—dc20 91-30151
CIP

For Bob Lascola and Diane Christian,
who were there when it mattered.

It is a condition which confronts us, not a theory.
Grover Cleveland

And thus Bureaucracy, the giant power wielded by pygmies, came into the world.
Balzac

Was it not Nixon who said, "Solutions are not the answer?"
Pat Paulson

There can be no whitewash at the White House.
Richard M. Nixon

The whole point of autocracy, Crispus observed, is that the accounts will not come right unless the ruler is their only auditor.
Tacitus

The immediate instruments are two: the motionless camera, and the printed word. The governing instrument—which is also one of the centers of the subject—is individual, anti-authoritative human consciousness.
James Agee

Contents

Foreword

by William M. Kunstler

Bruce Jackson is a longtime friend and one of his pieces in *Disorderly Conduct,* "The Indians of Attica," is about a case of mine. It occurred to me that this double connection might make it somewhat unseemly for me to introduce this splendid collection, but my concern quickly evanesced after I read or reread each of the eighteen pieces gathered here. Given their sublime and uniform excellence and enduring relevance, expression of my high regard for them seemed to me perfectly in order, so long as I made a full disclosure of the closeness of our relationship, which I now, quite proudly, do.

Many people before Bruce Jackson have written about these American matters but I can think of hardly any others who consistently manage to combine lucid description and narration with analysis that isn't grounded in cant. What I like about these essays, which cover an array of highly significant topics from peace demonstrations in the 1960s to contemporary federal drug policies, is that the politics and theory seem to *derive* from what their author saw; with most observers, the politics and theory seem to *control* what they saw. The result here is a rare measure of balance and clarity, a group of articles with remarkable currency. They are not only interesting as good writing and valid as pieces of history, but they provide ways for us to look at what is going on now in, say, the current "war" on drugs, and recent events in China, Eastern Europe, and the Persian Gulf.

I particularly liked that the book begins and ends with examinations of the claim to truth. Most people who offer us a collection of their articles say, in essence, "Here's what I thought about this and that," or "Here's what I saw." Bruce provides us with another dimension: he lets us in on the writer's side of the critical questions about truth and validity that are central to this kind of literature.

We live in an age when an astonishing amount of claptrap is proffered as revealed knowledge by anyone with a word processor and a willing publisher. I find it delightfully refreshing to find so articulate an olio of intelligent and searching pieces that are as articulate as they are provocative. And, happily, Bruce Jackson has been blessed with the gift of laughter, which helps him deliver to us a remarkably sane vision of a world that all too often is more than a little mad.

Acknowledgments

The following publishers granted permission to print previously published material:

Anonym for "Finding the Topknot" (no. 5/6, 1970, pp. 103–13). A much shorter version with some theoretical considerations appears as the "Postscript" to *A Thief's Primer* (New York: Macmillan, 1969), pp. 237–43.

Atlantic Monthly for "Who Goes to Prison: Caste and Careerism in Crime" (January 1966, pp. 52–57), "White-Collar Pill Party" (August 1966, pp. 35–40), "Exiles from the American Dream" (January 1967, pp. 44–51), and "The Battle of the Pentagon" (January 1968, pp. 35–42).

Buffalo Spree for "It's Just Petty Violence, Sir" (19:3, Fall 1985, pp. 106–27).

Cornell University Press for "Deviance as Success: The Double Inversion of Stigmatized Roles," which appeared in Barbara Babcock, ed., *The Reversible World: Symbolic Inversion in Art and Society* (Ithaca, N.Y., 1978, pp. 258–75).

Journal of American Folklore for "What People Like Us Are Saying When We Say We're Saying the Truth" (101:401, 1988, pp. 276–92) and "The Perfect Informant" (103:410, 1990, pp. 400–416).

Nation for "The Indians of Attica: A Taste of White Man's Justice" (10 May 1975, pp. 562–64).

New Republic for "Blackballing the Fiedlers" (9 September 1967, pp. 13–14).

New York Times for "The Drug Czar's Ideas Are a Bust: Going through These Things Twice" (Op-ed page, 3 April 1989).

Texas Monthly for "Hard Time" (6:12, December 1978, pp. 138–43, 255–63).

transAction/Society for "In the Valley of the Shadows: Kentucky" (8:8, June 1971, pp. 28–38), "Devil's Island Redux" (19:5, July–August 1982, pp. 14–19), and "The Black Box of Criminal Bureaucracy" (22:6, September–October 1985, pp. 56–67).

Introduction: Being There

In early March 1991, three white officers of the Los Angeles Police Department clubbed and kicked Rodney Glen King, a twenty-five-year-old black man, for speeding. The event was observed by twenty-one other department officers and two California Highway Patrol officers, including the sergeant charged with supervising the three officers brutalizing King; none of the officers in that group interfered with the beating. The three kicked King at least six times and struck him with nightsticks at least fifty-six times; they also shot him twice with a Taser electric stun gun. King's skull was fractured in nine places, his eye socket was shattered, one of his legs was broken, and he suffered severe nerve damage likely to result in partial paralysis.

The highest recorded speed in the chase that resulted in his mutilation was 55 m.p.h., although initial reports claimed a 110-m.p.h. pursuit (see Mydans 1991). What kept this from being one more reckless driving and resisting arrest case was a citizen across the street who happened to be testing his new camcorder. The beating was documented and the event became the most notorious case of police brutality since Bull Connor set police dogs on peaceful antisegregation marchers in Birmingham, Alabama, in 1964.

The same night the Rodney Glen King footage was broadcast, President George Bush made a speech to Congress about his grand triumph over Iraq. While waiting for Bush to enter the House chamber, a reporter said that the Democrats in Congress had learned only a short time earlier that the Republicans had all been given small American flags to wave at appropriate moments; the Democratic leadership, in a burst of last-minute activity, managed to acquire enough flags for their side of the aisle. During the broadcast, only a few senators and representatives seemed unwilling to enter into the carnival atmosphere. In his speech George Bush told us that we were entering a New World Order.

When, in the same late-night news summary, I again saw the videotape of the white cops torturing Rodney Glen King and George Bush telling us that we were approaching a New World Order, I knew that the essays in this collection possessed as much current interest as they ever did.

These essays are about life on the ground in America and the gritty side of public policy; they're also about the way we acquire and manage information having to do with these matters. Some of the essays deal with bureaucracy and enfranchisement: how power brokers in government agencies rationalize the way they divide up the world. Some are about day-to-day life a little beyond or below where middle-class Americans ordinarily hang out. And some are about what's going on when we try to tell one another what we saw out there. The earliest of the essays was published slightly over twenty-five years ago; the most recent is published here for the first time.

Most have to do with things I saw and people I knew, things like bayonets pointed at benign civilians on the Pentagon porch; miners and mine owners trying to get a piece of the dream in eastern Kentucky; the owner of a Mexican whorehouse and an American hustler discussing business and trading stories during an icy night in Nuevo Laredo; getting through the days in the toughest prison in Texas; narcotics cops in Harlem visiting a junkie with lunar-landscape abscess scars on his thighs; an upper-middle-class party where instead of booze the host served some of the best pharmaceutical dope commercially available; and the five large French windows in my living room exploding just before dawn on a summer morning.

As I suggested above, the older descriptive essays are not of historical interest only. Much of the misdirection, inefficiency, and self-interest I witnessed in drug-law enforcement and prison management in the sixties, seventies, and eighties is mirrored in the current federal approach to the crack problem. Too many politicians still capitalize on misery, and in the process they generate a lot of noise, spend a lot of money, do little good, and accomplish substantial harm. Our prison population has tripled in the past fifteen years (it is expected to pass one million not long after the turn of the century), and the problems of crowding, futility, abuse, and addled management still obtain. The conflict between the just limits of government power and the necessary extent of individual rights that was central in the antiwar demonstrations and the prison cases of the sixties and seventies is central to the right-to-life/pro-choice controversy and to recent Supreme Court cases that narrow the meaning of civil rights. Twenty-five years ago, politicians and businessmen diverted from the federal poverty program money intended to help the poor; during the Reagan administration, corrupt businessmen working with senior politicians in the Department of Housing and Urban Development likewise diverted housing money intended to help the poor. The players change, the rhetoric undergoes cosmetic reconfiguration, and the dance goes on.

II

I had occasion not long ago to show someone a photograph I'd taken of my friend Billy Lee Brammer in San Antonio in 1966. Billy Lee had been sort of raised by Sam Rayburn and Lyndon Johnson. He was a press aide to LBJ until 1961, when his novel, *The Gay Place,* was published, after which LBJ never spoke to him again. One of the protagonists of the novel is Arthur Fenstermaker, governor of an unnamed state that is part cattle-west and part cotton-south; Fenstermaker dies in bed with a Hollywood starlet. LBJ was a notorious screwer of starlets and anything else that moved. "What really hurt me," Billy Lee said of Johnson's rejection of him, "was I took out of the novel everything that made the sonofabitch the sonofabitch he was, but the sonofabitch got mad at me anyway." Billy Lee was forty-eight years old when he died of a drug overdose in 1978.

When I took the photograph, Billy Lee was thirty-six and I was thirty. The picture is still a good portrait of Billy Lee, but it's no longer the portrait of a man older than I. It's the Billy Lee Brammer I knew, but the *I* in that clause is a character in the past, not the *I* typing this sentence, which exists at this moment in time. It's more than a little astonishing, after all this time, to come back to Rimbaud's *"Car* Je *est un autre"—For* I *is another.* The *I* of the past is always a third-person character; the only first-person *I* is the one in the present tense.

I mention this because it explains why I haven't tinkered with these essays. In the past, when I read authors' justifications for not revising collections of previously published pieces, I assumed that the authors just didn't want to think about that old stuff any more. Now I realize that I misunderstood something important. I don't mind thinking about the reality behind these pieces or what I had to say in them (though sometimes I'd argue with the author), but there's no way the *I* that I am now can fairly edit what the *I* that I was then wrote.

If I tune the writing in my 1968 *Atlantic* piece on the antiwar demonstration at the Pentagon, I'm doing the tuning with the ear of a man twenty-three years older than the author of that article. Were I to take part in such a political demonstration now, I wouldn't see or hear or say or do the same things. I wouldn't come home with the same notes. To rework that article now, I'd have to impose on it a sensibility that couldn't have gotten the facts upon which the article is based, a sensibility that knows what came later: the 1968 Tet offensive, the student demonstrations following the U.S. incursions into Cambodia and killings at Kent State and Jackson State, America's loss of the Vietnam War and the subsequent attempt by the military and the government to place the blame on the press and the peace movement, the invasions of Grenada and Panama from which the press was almost entirely excluded, and the recent war for control of the oil fields of the Middle East in which the American press was almost perfectly controlled by all the governments involved. Better to leave things as they were, to swap what occasionally strikes me as an infelicity of prose for integrity of perception.

In the introductions to the individual articles I have provided some information on what happened later (when that mattered) and on the context of the writing. I'll ask you to bear with me through those moments when I used "one" instead of "I" and "*Weltanschauung*" instead of "worldview," when I used such locutions as "girl" for a woman in her twenties and "Negro" for someone we would now refer to as a "black" or "African-American," and when I cited examples of outdated technology such as a Super-8 camera rather than an 8-mm high-band camcorder. I'll also ask you to make your own conversions about money matters to take inflation into account. In "Blackballing the Fiedlers," for example, I refer to a comfortable neighborhood of "$25,000–$50,000 homes"; those same houses now go for well over $250,000. New York detectives now make a good deal more than the detective in "Exiles from the American Dream" who says that the $420 a week spent by a junkie informant on drugs is "almost what I make a month."

What I really mean is, some of the diction and a bit of the technology in the earlier pieces may be dated, but I am certain that their substance is still very much with us.

Disorderly Conduct

The Perfect Informant

(Journal of American Folklore, 1990)

I never had any doubt regarding that old conundrum about the falling tree in the forest: of course it makes a sound, whether or not anyone is there to listen. The real question is, Does the sound it makes matter if no person or animal is there to listen? Probably not.

Researchers and journalists ask people out there a lot of questions. For a range of reasons we try to get them to tell us their stories. What we often forget in the process is that the people whose words we're writing down or tape-recording have their own reasons for talking to us, and those reasons often have nothing whatsoever to do with our notions of why we're both occupying that space at that time and engaging in that conversation. As with the sound of the falling tree, stories need two participants to occur. Without the receptor, the story is just waves in the air or bits of ink on a page. What I learned in the course of writing this article is that the experience isn't passive; it's collaborative, even symbiotic.

The conversations that form the substance of this article are based on my notes, some of which are more detailed than others. I sometimes don't know until later what's really important, so my field notes may provide sketchy information on what mattered most and a great deal of detail about what turned out to have been of marginal significance. As you'll learn shortly, what I thought was going on in this series of encounters wasn't what was going on at all, and what I was focusing on as subject was only evidence of the real subject, like the ionized track in a Wilson cloud chamber telling you where a radioactive particle just was. I don't think I recreated the gist of any of these conversations, but you should take them the way you would if we were walking around the block and I were telling you a personal experience story rather than the way you might if you were in a jury box and I were a witness testifying under oath. If I *were* testifying under oath and if the cross-examiner asked, "Are those the *exact* words, Mr. Jackson?" I would respond, "Maybe, maybe not, but that's what we *said.*"

Je t'apporte l'enfant d'une nuit d'Idumée!
(I bring you the child of an Idumean night!)

Stéphane Mallarmé,
"Don du poème"

Stewart's Call

MY FRIEND STEWART[1] called one fine autumn day a few years ago. "Are you still working on that book about oral histories from the Vietnam War?" I told him that I'd left the project for a while to do other things and that I'd never gotten back to it. "Well," Stewart said, "I've got someone who wants to meet you. When you meet him, you may find yourself back in it again."

Not likely, I told him, not likely at all. For one thing, Diane Christian and I were deep in the editing of a film, a job that would consume most of our non-teaching time for the next several months. And there were other projects and commitments: obligations were stacked up like planes at O'Hare. There were other reasons, but I didn't tell Stewart what they were.

I'd begun the research for the oral history book in 1976. I thought it would be useful to record how veterans were remembering the war and what they had to say about coming home. I'd done enough personal narrative research to know that reality is rewritten constantly by memory and that the further you are from the event the further you are from any accurate redaction of it. The stories would change over time, as is the way of stories in active tradition, so it would be good to have some baseline narratives. The project really should have begun five or six years earlier, but back then I was too deep in antiwar activities to have thought of or been able to do anything like that.

The politics of which-side-are-you-on were pretty much over by 1976. Former war resisters were beginning to learn that the vets weren't the guys who had kept the war going all those pointless years, and the vets had already tired of defending a war that made sense in no terms other than sunk costs. It was hard to write off the antiwar movement as subversive and the vets as a group of right-wing militaristic thugs (in part because Ron Kovic and people like him were blowing those stereotypes away). I thought we'd be at least as long coming to terms with the emotional residue of that war as we would the economic burdens it imposed on us and our children. So the interviews were both feasible and reasonable.

The interviews were mostly free form, but there was a small group of questions I asked nearly every time, each of which produced long and involved answers. One was, "What did you do in Vietnam?" Most men would answer, "What do you mean by *do*?" to which I'd shrug or say, "I don't know. Whatever you think it means." And then they'd take some meaning of *do* and hang a bunch of narratives on it. Another question was "What happened when you came home?" To which several said, "What happened in what regard?" to which I'd also shrug or say "I don't know," and that would occasion another narrative or string of narratives.

Lydia Fish, a friend at a nearby college, was teaching a class called "The Vietnam Experience." She asked me to talk to her students, nearly all of whom were Vietnam vets, about the antiwar movement at home. She said I would find the visit interesting because I wouldn't have to prepare a formal talk and the class had a pattern of a lot of vigorous give and take. She was an old pal so I said okay, expecting a lot of flak.

But the flak didn't come. Maybe it was that the war was by then long enough in the past or because I was a vet from another time or because some of the men in the class knew me from when I ran for Congress in 1968 as an antiwar candidate. In the course of the discussion, one of them said something like, "In World War II and in Korea, people went over as a unit and stayed together as a unit and came back as a unit. And the going and coming took a long time. With us, we went alone, stayed a year, and came home alone."

"If you made it through the year," someone else said.

A third man said, "You got to understand the feeling you get when you're in the 'Nam one day and the next day you're in San Francisco airport getting spat on by an old lady or a hippie."

"That happened to *you*?"

"A buddy of mine."

This anecdote had turned up more frequently than any other in my interviews. The first few times I heard it I had marveled at the rudeness of the old lady and the stupidity of the hippie. I mean, you have to be crazy to spit on a guy just out of the jungle. I'd ask, "What did you do when that happened?" and invariably I got a vague answer. I began pushing: "A hippie spat on *you*?" and the answers were like those that came up in Lydia's class:

"Well, not me, exactly. A good buddy of mine. It happened to him."

So I asked Lydia's students: "How many people in this room had a buddy who was spat upon by an old lady or a hippie or something like that?"

Maybe a third of the hands went up.

"How many people in this room were spat upon themselves?"

No hands went up.

"Don't you think that's odd—that one out of three people in this room has a pal that it happened to but it didn't happen to anybody here? I mean, if you guys are at all representative, and I'm sure you are, then it happened to a large percentage of men coming home through San Francisco. So how come it didn't happen to any of you?"

"It happened to some guys we know," someone said.

"Yeah," someone else said.

"What's your *point?*" someone else said.

I told them that my point was that stories weren't just facts, they were also strategies, that when people told them to one another when they were hanging out it was okay to just listen and come back with your own, but when we talked about them in a classroom situation we ought to be looking behind the narration for the reasons a particular story has a particular power. While I was talking to them I understood for the first time what the story was really about: in addition to the personal experience narratives that each man used to manage his own past, there was also a group of shared narratives that were taken on as if they were personal experiences. The lie was that it happened to the teller; the truth too hard to articulate was that the stories were a way of containing a desperate need.

After the class, several of them invited me to join them at the campus bar. We closed the place, drinking beer and telling stories. Later, I interviewed some men from the class. They were similar to the other interviews I'd done.

I started wondering if some kinds of narratives in my interviews were as common as they seemed or if something I was doing was eliciting those kinds of narratives rather than others. That is, I wondered if I was finding real patterns or if I was finding what I wanted to find. So I prepared a list of what had developed as my basic outline questions and asked several friends in various parts of the country to do a few interviews using those questions as starting points. Some were done by men, some by women; some were done by Vietnam vets, some by people who had never been on a military base; some were done by people who thought the war an evil America had imposed on the world, some were done by people who thought the war had been a noble enterprise. Though they were different in detail, the contours of these interviews were similar to mine. I thought I was on the right track.

I was heading toward an easy book that would probably sell very well, but it just didn't feel right. I was uncomfortable because it seemed that I had an opportunistic relationship with the narratives: I was gathering fascinating material without much real effort or engagement or danger. I'm no Puritan; I don't think good things have to be painful to be deserved—but this wasn't close to painful. It was fieldwork on autopilot.

Then Diane and I got to know a couple whose only son had been killed by his own artillery fire the week he'd been due to come home. The father wanted us to do a book about what happened. We told him that a book already existed, *Friendly Fire,* and it was a very good book. "This is different," the father said. "What's different is it happened to you," I told him. "Just read the letters," he said. I did. I read all the letters the boy wrote his parents and his girlfriend. Some were interesting, some were poignant in light of what happened, and most were the kind of letters a kid far from home writes the people who are grounding him in the world. They reminded me of letters I had written home when I'd been in the marines 25 years earlier. I told the man I couldn't do his book for him.

And I realized I couldn't do mine either: I just hadn't earned it. I abandoned the project. I didn't even transcribe most of the tapes.

That's how I reconstruct it now, but my motives maybe weren't all that pure at the time. A good deal of material about Vietnam vets had begun to appear about then, and perhaps I thought that by the time I got through with all I had to do, the subject would be used up, stale, old news. Even my working title had appeared as the title of a successful Jane Fonda movie, "Coming Home." The Vietnam War experience had become trendy: racist fantasy films by Chuck Norris were making megabucks around the world (the U.S. government couldn't get the POWs out or even convince itself that there *were* POWs; Norris, in his films, did both) and the Vietnam War was on network TV as sentimental background for programs like "Magnum, P.I." and "Simon and Simon."

That's why the tapes were packed in boxes. Someday, maybe, I'd get back to them. Or they'd have some archival value. Something. But not now, not me now.

Jim Bennett

That's where things were when my friend Stewart called. "It's a student," Stewart said, "he's read your books and he wants to meet you. He was in Special Forces in Vietnam, then he came back to the States for Officer's Candidate School and he came across your stuff while he was in OCS in Texas. Then he went back to Vietnam in Special Forces as an officer. He made captain, was discharged with disability; he's got several major decorations. Now he's a student here getting a degree and he's helping me on my research project. He's a terrific guy. And he told me that one of the reasons he came here was he hoped to meet you."

I'm no more capable of resisting a line like that than you. "Oh," I said, "in that case, set something up."

"Don't have to," he said. "He's coming to the screening of *Death Row* at the college Friday." *Death Row* was a film Diane and I had made several years earlier about men waiting to be executed in Texas.

Stewart found us in the lobby after the screening. With him was a thin, wiry man in his thirties. He introduced himself: "Hi, I'm Jim Bennett and I've been wanting to meet you for a long time. When I was in the special army program at University of Texas one of the teachers assigned us *A Thief's Primer* and I thought it was a fantastic book. You really got into that guy's world. I'd like to do something like that someday with some of the people I know." He said that when Stewart had assigned the book earlier in the term he'd been delighted at the coincidence, and then when he'd learned that Stewart was a friend of mine he'd asked him to arrange an introduction. He'd been through a great deal, he said, and he hoped to be able to write about it someday. He wondered if—he knew I was a very busy man and I shouldn't be at all embarrassed if I had to say no—if I'd be willing to talk to him some time about doing fieldwork, about interviewing, about going from fieldwork to printed documents.

"I was working on some Vietnam vet interviews," I said, "but it wasn't right. Maybe you can do the book I bailed out of."

"Maybe," he said, "and that's what I'd like to talk to you about. How about it?"

This was a perfect delight: what better way to get myself off the hook maintained by those unutilized interviews than to pass it on to someone with far more right to the material than I?

Over the next month we met three or four times. Jim came to dinner and we talked deep into the night. Mostly it was war stories. Some of the stories were like stories I'd heard in my interviews, some were entirely new to me, and some reminded me of stories I'd heard from old salts who'd been in Korea a little too long. We got deep really fast because, I think, it was like the conversation was already in progress when we joined it for the first time.

Jim telephoned early one morning. "How'd you like to meet General Westmoreland?" There was, he said, a luncheon with the general before his talk at the state college later in the week. About thirty people would be going and he had reserved tickets for us.

I'd just read Westmoreland's autobiography, *A Soldier Reports* (1972), an astonishing rationalization of military disaster. Westmoreland was still blaming civilians back home for the failure of the American war in Vietnam he directed. He hadn't understood then why he was losing and he couldn't admit now why he had lost. His only triumph was in a slander suit against CBS. During the years of his command our troop commitment expanded geometrically, frequently on the basis of promises by him that if he were sent only this or that many more young bodies he'd take care of the commies in no time.

"You still there?" Jim said.

I told him I had been thinking about something. I said some vile things about Westmoreland.

"If you feel that strongly," Jim said, "then you certainly should come. See what you're so angry at."

Couldn't argue that, so I said we'd meet him down at the Waterfront Hilton. We did. Westmoreland, dressed in a conservative blue suit, was a good deal smaller than I'd expected. Most of the army publicity photos of him must have been taken from fairly low angles. He talked briefly about the grand mission they'd all been part of over there and said how much he respected and thanked them every one and how much he missed the boys who didn't make it back. There were communal feelings and great applause. The rest of the luncheon was pleasant enough, though it reminded me of the scene in *Night of the Generals* when the homicidal Nazi played by Peter O'Toole is to address the surviving former members of his SS battalion.

Jim moved close to Westmoreland and introduced himself. He reminded the general of the time Westmoreland had come to a line outfit to visit the troops and Jim had been there. "I was just a lieutenant then," Jim said. He told the general what his nickname had been. Westmoreland brightened, said he remembered, shook Jim's hand enthusiastically. Jim introduced us. Westmoreland shook our hands enthusiastically. Then he moved on, shaking other hands, happy with people who understood him. "Great guy," Jim said, "and he's got a great memory. He remembers everybody." Later he told us that everyone in 'Nam had a nickname. "That made it easier for everyone else when someone got killed, and it made it easier coming home because it was easier separating yourself from what you did over there. At least for some guys. It was good for me that way."

A few weeks later, Jim called to say he had something that would interest me. "You use a Nikon, right?"

"Leica mostly. But I have Nikons."

"Well, I'm asking about the Nikons. I got a night scope that fits on a Nikon lens. You can take pictures in matchlight from a thousand feet. You can read lips in starlight. The CIA developed it. You can fit it on a movie camera too. Fantastic. We used them in 'Nam for nighttime sniping. But you can use it for anything. Look around at the other cars in the drive-in, for instance."

"I don't go to drive-ins."

"With this lens, it might be interesting going to drive-ins."

He had two of them, he said, and he'd let me have one for as long as I wished.

Jim knew, as did anyone who spent much time around my house, that I loved gadgets that did things. I have no interest in gadgets for their own sake, but anything that is functional, no matter how complex, I'm delighted to try until I decide if it will be useful or silly. I told him that I'd seen a "60 Minutes" segment the previous week in which they had used just that sort of device for some terrific nighttime shots of malefactors. "Oh yeah," he said, "I think I caught that show."

He didn't have the scope when he came over for dinner a few days later. He'd meant to bring it, he said, but he'd forgotten it because he'd decided to tell me about a project he'd been thinking about for some time but had thus far hesitated to mention.

"Go ahead," I said. "What is it?"

"No," he said, "I don't want to impose."

"Don't be silly," I said.

"Well, it's about your project about guys coming home."

"My ex-project."

"I know. You told me. But I think you ought to do it. But not as a book. Do it as a movie. There's lots of guys I can introduce you to, some of them living in the bush, some of them who wouldn't ever talk to anyone else, and you can do a film about what it was like for them coming back then and what it's like for them now. Not just guys: there's some nurses you ought to meet. See, for a lot of us, it's not over. It won't ever be over. And people don't know that. These are *interesting* guys. Interesting to me, anyway. But we'd have to travel to where some of them are and you probably don't have time for that."

The more reasons he gave for difficulty, the more interested I became. By the end of that visit I was making notes about possible funding sources. We'd interview and follow with our camera men and women in New York, Texas, Montana, California, and New Mexico. Some had jobs and families; some lived like jungle rats. The location work would take months and editing would be a monstrous job but, we all agreed, it would be worth it.

The matter of credits came up. Jim said he didn't care about credits, he just wanted to do the job. Diane and I said he had to be either director or producer. His contacts, after all, would make the film possible, and his expertise on the post-Vietnam experience would provide the perspective. I think we wound up with Diane and me as producers, and Jim as director. We would apply for the grants jointly, with the three of us as project directors, him the expert on war and us the experts on documentary film.

The next time he came over we talked about funding possibilities for the film. He again didn't have the scope with him. I didn't say anything about it because I didn't want Jim to think that I was interested in him only for what he could give me, like information and nifty devices. That is, I didn't want him to know what was pretty much the truth: without the war information and without the devices, we didn't have much to talk about and we sure wouldn't have been pals. (Every fieldwork relationship has that measure of using one another to it, I think, and the important thing is making sure that it's at least reasonably bilateral.) We talked about the film. Diane had talked to someone at NEH to see if there was a possibility it might fit one of their funding programs. Jim said he thought we could get money from some corporations that had highly placed vets in management, like Federal Express. "I can get the names and addresses of those people," Jim said. "No problem at all."

We made preliminary budget notes. Film, processing, travel, equipment. Salaries, one of which was for him for a year. I asked how much he wanted. He said a number, I no longer remember what it was, but I do remember that it was far too low. I doubled it. "Oh," he said, "do you really think that's a reasonable amount?"

"Sure," I said.

"Well," he said, "all right then. I guess it's okay."

After he left, Diane said, "I don't think he was satisfied with the salary we put him in there for." I reminded her that it was double what he'd put himself in for. "Yes," she said, "but I had a feeling he was just being modest or something, that he knew perfectly well he was asking for too little, that he expected us to kick it up. And I don't think we went as far as he wanted."

"Maybe you're right. I'll increase it another fifty percent. How's that?"

"Fine with me," she said. "But you should check with Jim."

I did. I called him the next day, said Diane and I had been going over the budget and we'd decided his salary was still too low for someone of his expertise and experience, especially given his centrality to the project. "So we'll boost it another fifty percent."

"Fifty percent more on what I proposed or on what you proposed?"

"On what we proposed."

"Good," he said, "that *is* okay."

Jim said he had been trained in the whole panoply of infantry weapons, but he had specialized in those that were silent, especially the crossbow. He was known, everywhere among the Green Berets, he said, as the expert with the crossbow. He was also, he said, an expert in the use of nitroglycerine. I'd never heard of military people using nitro. When I'd been in the marines we'd had plastique and I'd received a little training in its use. I knew that there were stronger versions of plastique around during Vietnam. "Why nitro?" I asked him. "Why not plastique?"

"Because plastique has to be made in a factory and you need to fuse it somehow. Nitro, if you don't have it, you can make it. They taught us how to make it. Just like with the crossbow: they taught us how to make that too. So if you're caught out somewhere, you're not defenseless. You can do 'em anywhere," he said.

One time he'd been on assassination mission with his crossbow and after the kill he'd been separated from the others in his unit and then wounded. He holed up in enemy territory for several days until he could make his way back. His wound infected. He treated the infection using a folk remedy he'd learned from a Buddhist monk: he got maggots from a dead animal and put them into his wound. He had no anesthetic. "Maggots are nature's way of keeping the world clean," he said with terrific equanimity. Diane asked if it didn't hurt terribly. Jim shrugged. The shrug said: These are the kinds of things men like us endure.

He told us in great detail about the respect everyone had for the monks. "You could be in a terrific firefight," he said, "and a line of those saffron monks would come out of the bush and walk across the clearing and go into the bush on the other side. The whole time they were there, all the firing stopped. Nobody said anything. It was just what everybody did. And then when they were gone, the firing started up again like nothing had happened."

"Why did the Communists stop shooting?" Diane asked.

"Because the monks were holy men. Doesn't have anything to do with communism or anything else."

Jim told us he was involved in the CIA's Phoenix Project—assassination of village officials with supposed VC connections. "Not just the officials," Jim said. "Their wives and children and goats and chickens. Everything died." He didn't like talking about that phase of his experience, he said. Maybe another time. He told us that since he was attached to CIA for that part of his tour, his work was so secret that false military records were made as cover and for deniability later. Even his DD214, his official discharge document, covered up his real assignments. "You look at it," he said, "and you wouldn't know I was in 'Nam or that I was wounded twice or anything. The only way you can see my real records is if you got top secret clearance, and even that might not do it." It was the secret nature of his assignments during his second tour in Vietnam, he said, that was the cause of his problems with the Veterans Administration. He had been trying to get disability payments for the lung disorder resulting from the time he'd been doused with Agent Orange when he'd been on recon. "Those pilots couldn't have known we were that far north," he said, so his gripe wasn't with them. The pilots were just doing their job, and a dangerous one it was; his gripe was with the VA, which wouldn't give him disability. They disallowed his claims because their version of his records didn't show him in Vietnam at all; they just showed him in Germany, which was his cover story. He said he was trying to get the people who control such things to declassify his records so he could get what was coming to him. He said it was really rotten that after all that had happened to him, he had to fight so hard to get his benefits.

Jim fell off a roof. I visited him in the hospital a few times. He told me war stories, talked about his job as a sheriff's deputy, told me again about how he had come across one of my books while he'd been in the special officer's training program at University of Texas. He said his lung problems and improper healing of some old wounds weren't making getting over the fall any easier. Then we talked more about the project.

Jim got out of the hospital and I visited him at home. Several of the guys from the local vets' organization were there. They told stories about people at school, not much about the war. One of the guys said, "Say, Jim, you through with my medals? My wife, she's after me to get them back."

"Oh, sure," Jim said.

Someone else said, "If you're doing that, I'd like my CIB, if you're done with it."

"No problem," Jim said. He got out of the chair with obvious difficulty and limped into the bedroom. He came out with several framed medals. I couldn't see them all, but I made out a Silver Star, Bronze Star, Purple Heart. And he held an unmounted Combat Infantryman's Badge.

The guy with the medals left and the others went into the kitchen for more beer. While they were gone, I asked Jim, "How come you had their medals?"

"Oh, mine got lost in one of those moves and Alice [his girlfriend] and some other people wanted to see what they looked like."

One of those moves. I had no idea what moves he was talking about, but it seemed a minor point so I didn't pursue it.

I looked around to see if I could spot the night scopes, but they weren't anywhere in sight. This didn't seem an appropriate time to ask for one of them and Jim never raised the issue.

Bud Johns, a friend in San Francisco, called to say hello, and that was the night things with Bennett began to unravel. Bud told us what was going on with him and we told him what was going on with us. One of those conversations you have with distant pals once or twice a year to keep the lines open so when you do manage a visit there isn't an inordinate amount of catching up to do. We told him about Jim.

"He sounds fantastic," Bud said.

"He is," I said.

"So why do you believe him?"

"What do you mean? Why shouldn't we believe him?"

"I don't know," Bud said, "but you might at least give it some thought, and it doesn't sound like you've done that yet."

While Diane chatted with Bud I began going over what I'd said to him thus far. I'd told him at least a half-dozen terrific Jim Bennett stories. There weren't many people about whom I could repeat so many stories so easily—and that's what Bud responded to and it's what I now, for the first time, began thinking about critically. Everything he told us was so spectacular. So many great stories. And there he was, just waiting to meet *me.* I had been so pleased that he'd been waiting to meet me that I never considered the improbability of such a desire: *why* should a guy between combat tours going through OCS in Texas want to meet a professor in Buffalo? Sure, it was a possibility, but it wasn't likely. Just as each of those other stories was a possibility, but in contiguity they weren't likely.

Before joining Levi Strauss, Bud had been a newspaper reporter for many years. When Diane put me back on the phone I told him that he'd probably ruined my evening and that I thought his old journalistic cynicism was coming out. "Maybe," he said, "but I wouldn't call it cynicism. Caution is what I'd call it. I always preferred finding out a story was wrong before it got printed than afterwards." He gave me an avuncular lecturette on checking the facts, especially the ones that are so good they're almost too good to be true. I asked if that were more newsman's savvy. "No," he said, "I got that from a Dashiell Hammett story."

I hung up the phone and said to Diane, "Bud's a cynical bastard."

"I know," she said.

"I think he may be right."

"I know," she said.

We began going over the coincidences in Jim's various stories and also the things that didn't get delivered, like the night scope, which I was now convinced had never existed, and the records that couldn't be found or were so secret they couldn't be shown. I said that I thought it weird that someone's military records were so secret that he'd have difficulty getting medical attention from the VA.

"It's worse than weird," Diane said.

It was the nitro, and the Langvei story, that brought him down.

Jim told about the time his Special Forces camp in Langvei had been overrun by tanks and fried with napalm. The Americans hadn't known the VC *had* tanks or napalm, he said, so they weren't ready for it either. Nearly everyone was killed. The survivors barely made it to the Marine base at Khe Sanh, which at that time was in the middle of its major assault of the war.

Something was vaguely familiar about the story and I said so. "Sure," Jim said, "anyone who was in Special Forces knows about it." I wasn't in Special Forces so Jim's explanation didn't satisfy. Later, I recounted the conversation to Lydia Fish. Lydia said, "It's not just Special Forces vets who know the story. Anyone who's read Michael Herr's *Dispatches* knows it. Herr tells it really well."[2]

A Special Forces vet heard Jim tell the story several times, and after a while something in the narration didn't ring right to him. He called the Special Forces Association in Washington. "The guy there said only a dozen guys came out of that battle and he knew the names of every one of them and Jim Bennett wasn't one of the names." That wasn't all: SFA had no listing for anyone named Jim Bennett ever having served in Special Forces at any rank. Someone else asked a colonel pal now based in the Pentagon to look into the matter of Bennett's service. The colonel checked the names of all men above the rank of warrant officer who had served in Southeast Asia; he found no record of anyone named Jim Bennett. What if Bennett had been doing top secret work, our friend asked the colonel, would his records be hidden from you now? This, the colonel said, is the one place the records would not be hidden. "This is where we do the hiding."

I wasn't there for the nitro fiasco, but Stewart was. Jim was going on about his nitro expertise and some guy he didn't know, who was sitting on the edge of the group and apparently hardly paying attention at all, looked at the ground and said in a flat voice, "You're full of shit, Bennett."

"What are you talking about, man?"

"I said you're full of shit. There wasn't any nitro in 'Nam."

"Damn right there was. And lots of it too."

"No. No, there wasn't. There wasn't any at all. Nitro is unstable over 85° and in 'Nam it didn't hardly ever go *under* 85°. You take nitro off ice and it blows up. No way you could take it into the bush 'less you took a truckload of ice too. So that's why you're full of shit. I don't think you ever were in 'Nam."

Later, Stewart told me that some of the men in the veterans' group had figured Jim for a phony several months before it all unraveled and that one had seen some official records that said Jim had spent his entire overseas time in Germany and that he'd left the military under a cloud. He asked one of the group's leaders why they didn't say anything. "He was doing such a good job calling campus attention to veterans' problems," the vet said, "that we thought we'd wait a while."

Not long ago I ran into a vet who had been in my classes some years ago, a fellow who was still around the fringes of the university trying to get a degree. He is less crazy than when I'd first known him, but he still is a spooky guy. I asked him if he had known Bennett. "Sure," he said. I asked if he'd known that Bennett was a phony. "Sure," he said. He'd been a Green Beret himself and he'd been at one or two of the places Jim said he'd been, so he knew Jim was making it up.

"Why didn't you ever blow the whistle on him?"

"Wasn't doing me any harm. And he told such great stories. I loved listening to him tell those goddamned stories. I mean, I was *there* and I couldn't tell stories like that guy."

Substitute Lives

I've told you about a project that didn't happen, about how my own desire for a project with meaning let me ignore meaningful facts already in my field of view, how it took the intuitive remark of a transcontinental pal in the course of a casual telephone call to start turning on the daylight.

I'd felt like a fool, but at least I'd learned something: it's not enough just to think about how you can execute your project; you've also got to think about your investment in the project and evaluate how that investment may be ordering the way you're looking at the things of this world. Faustus went all the way, but we're making deals with our devils too. I don't know if we ever really win, but I do know that if we're not aware of the compromises, the negotiations, of the battle to achieve some vision that goes beyond our own interests, we're sure to lose. Or betray.

I was still running on ego and emotion. I was still thinking about it all in terms of myself, how I'd been deceived because I'd been complicit in the enacted narrative. It wasn't until I sat down to write this essay that the second realization hit, and it too was about a failed inquiry. The first resulted from Jim's scam and my willingness to be complicit in it; the second resulted from my willingness to let it end there.

Because the end of that project that didn't happen was really and already the middle of another one that did, an inquiry for which I already had a good deal of data: not the story of the heroes, but the others, those who are so desperate to acquire the reality of another they gather up and process more folklore than any folklorist ever could or would. Had Jim's stories been only true, I would have been involved in a project of obvious interest; had I been cool or smart or objective enough to look at the story Jim and I were both enacting, I would have been led to something that dealt not with stories told but with the telling of stories, a study not in texts but in the profound feelings that make texts necessary and useful.

Jim, by the way, wasn't unique. Since that misadventure, I've since heard of numerous men who went to extraordinary lengths to convince people they had seen combat in Vietnam, and who were astonishingly successful at their deceptions. There was, for example, Jeffrey "Mad Dog" Beck, a broker with Drexel Burnam Lambert,

> decorated for heroism as a special forces platoon leader in Vietnam, rumored to have worked for the Central Intelligence Agency. No one, friends say, can make fighting in the steaming jungles of Southeast Asia come alive as can Mr. Beck, who has held many a Manhattan dinner party in thrall with his wartime tales. He likes to pull up his left shirtsleeve, point to a scar on his wrist and explain how it was shattered by a bullet from an AK-47 rifle during fighting in the Ia Drang Valley; only a bulky Seiko watch, Mr. Beck says grimly, saved his hand. For calling in napalm strikes on his own patrols and other exploits, he tells rapt listeners, he earned a Silver Star, two Bronze Stars and four Purple Hearts. [Burrough 1990:A1]

Beck became involved with Michael Douglas, who planned a movie based on Beck's life. He became friends with and consultant to director Oliver Stone. "The only problem," Burrough writes, "is that the banker's stories are almost all lies. A reporter's investigation into the star deal-maker's career reveals that much of Mr. Beck's 'past' has been created from whole cloth, the product, friends and business associates say, of the banker's active fantasy life." Burrough's "army records and his first wife's family confirm that he never served in the special forces, never fought in Vietnam, never, in fact, came closer to combat than the Army reserves." Like Jim Bennett, Beck claimed the discrepancies between his stories and his official records resulted from his having been an intelligence agent (Burrough, 1990:A1).

In the summer of 1989, a Salt Lake City man named Robert Fife committed suicide at the age of 46 and left behind a 449-page manuscript that detailed his experiences as a POW in Vietnam. He had been seeing a therapist who had been treating him for post-traumatic stress syndrome related to his time as a prisoner of war. Twenty years earlier, his wife's

> sneakers seemed to drive [him] berserk. He told her that his captors wore sneakers when they came to his cage to beat him and urinate on him and that the enemy soldier he strangled to escape was wearing sneakers.

> Robert Fife had a certificate, purportedly from the U.S.S. Ranger Committee, listing medals he said he burnt to protest bad treatment of Vietnam veterans. They included the Navy Cross.
>
> The certificate, which appeared to have been signed by Adm. Thomas H. Moorer, retired Chief of Naval Operations, said Lieut. (j.g.) Robert J. Fife, who had flown 130 missions over enemy territory, was "one of only four naval aviators to escape from enemy prison camps."

After his suicide, Fife's wife attempted to have his name included on Utah's Vietnam War memorial. Shortly before it was engraved, she learned that it was all a sham: Fife had been in the military for only eight months after his September 1965 enlistment. He had been given a medical discharge because a childhood injury to bones in his right foot had never healed property, and the only decoration he received was the Defense Service Award, which had been given to everyone in uniform ("Dead 'War Hero' Unmasked," *New York Times,* 1989).

A con man I once knew told me, "It takes two people to run a con. Somebody like me and somebody who wants it to happen. I'm the realist; he's the dreamer." Jim Bennett, Jeffrey Beck, Robert J. Fife, and others like them may have been dreamers when it came to their careers in Vietnam, but when it came to managing most of the people with whom they came into contact, they were the realists. They created the pasts they preferred to their own, and they got a number of highly educated people acting in terms of their creations.

I think one reason I wasn't critical earlier of Jim's stories and self-critical of my own motives in listening to them was that Jim fit perfectly the kind of narrator I wanted to hear at that time. His stories were rich in detail and visual in imagination; as he talked, I knew his stories would work well on a printed page. The political content of his stories let me be involved in a political rapprochement I don't think I sought but which I welcomed when it appeared: we could do something about the vileness of the Vietnam War without at the same time disparaging the sacrifice of the people who, for whatever reason, suffered there. It gave me a chance to do something with or at least partially grounded in all those earlier interviews, that uncompleted, unresolved inquiry occupying boxes of tapes, piles of transcription folders. And probably, at a deeper and more personal level, the conversations and rapport with Jim (whose military years were almost exactly halfway between the present and my own military years) provided a middle-aged professor a secondhand but nonetheless welcome connection to his own distant and romanticized youth.

If I had designed the perfect informant for this project, the informant I would have designed would have been Jim. Jim sensed my need and he gave me what I wanted. He was able to do that because, for reasons very much his own, he already had cast and directed himself in the role he had long readied himself to play. In addition to all the other mistakes I made in our discussions about the project was who was going to occupy what role: Jim was director all right. He was also producer and one of the principal actors. I was another actor, and also part of the audience.

But why did he bother? What were his reasons for this elaborate deception?

I don't think you can ever fully know someone else's motives; you only know for sure what they do. Jim was a terrific collector and processor of stories. He listened to people, he read, and then he began to tell. If he had a way of telling the story in the third person, he would have been Homeric, or at least a novelist; because he had no venue for such narrative he was instead pathologic. His need wasn't to find a good story in someone else's life, rather it was to find a good story for his own, and since his own experience didn't provide that, he set about expropriating the narratives of other people. Instead of becoming a successful social scientist or reporter he became a fraud. He was brilliant at creating venues in which he could recite his stories. He was self-creative, not self-destructive, as evidenced by the protective devices he tried to set up, such as the story about his secret records and his avoidance of being tape-recorded. My friend Stewart, who had become deeply involved with Jim in a long-term research project, provided one kind of listener and offered one set of opportunities; I provided another. Working with the two of us, Jim accumulated power of a kind: he was a central coordinator of Stewart's research project and he was going to be director of our film. He became a big shot in one of the local veterans' organizations. The stories got some of the war heroes he fervently wished he had been to accept him as one of their own; they also got academics who controlled or influenced resources to steer resources his way. None of that would have happened on the basis of having been an enlisted man doing menial work in Europe.

But what a curious narrative he devised! Jim designed a minefield, then shredded his map and stomped straight across to the other side. I think he *knew* he had to blow up, that he'd be caught, and that he'd be propelled into the real world and branded as a phony, a liar, a sicko. He was dealing with gullible but not stupid people: the arithmetic was inevitable. Jim wasn't stupid either; it took real intelligence to absorb and retell all those extended narratives, to manipulate so many of us in so complex a scenario.

Here's my guess on Jim's real payoff: once he got found out, Jim Bennett became what he wanted to be more than anything else—a Vietnam war casualty. It didn't happen to him in Southeast Asia, but it came out of that war anyway. He created a wound that really was *his* own, a scar the authenticity of which none of us can or would deny. His Vietnam story was a lie, but the pathology revealed and the shame created by that lie are real. Jim Bennett may not be one of the honorably wounded, but he's one of the wounded nonetheless, and probably for him that's as close as he could get. Once he was exposed, there was no longer any dissonance between his imaginary and his real worlds, between his private and public selves, so he could, perhaps for the first time, relax perfectly.

For most of us, there is a murky area at the edge of experience that can be used to tune our narratives and enhance our understanding of real life moments. It's the place where it's okay to talk about getting spat on in the San Francisco airport by the hippie, where it's efficient to collapse what happened to you one year with what happened another, where it's comfortable to be cooler or smarter or more alert than anyone outside of movies and memory ever is. Jim Bennett went to the far side of that area, to a place where the narratives became a substitute for real life rather than a way of understanding it. Jim Bennett ran into a no-man's-land of the imagination and couldn't come back until we caught him there. When it happened, I thought we were finding him out; now, six years later, I think we were a rescue party.

That's what I think. I don't know what Jim thought, because after things fell apart we never talked again. Neither of us thought we had anything more to say to the other, and that was another error. We had lots more to talk about.

That describes Jim Bennett and maybe it describes Robert J. Fife and others like them; but it still doesn't explain them. Many, perhaps most, of us would like to have fair claim to pasts more glorious or romantic or heroic or interesting than the ones we happen to have accumulated. But we don't create a history and try to occupy the present that history would have warranted.

Like hell we don't. We all, each and every one of us, continually recreate ourselves. Accidents of fate or whims of the moment in the distant past become, with the fulfillment of the present, meaningful, and we see those accidents and whims in structures that, if they ever existed at all, were totally transparent to us at the time. We understand human affairs in terms of narrative, and the narrative of our lives is protean, forever subject to new depths or breadths of understanding, new configurations and alignments of parts that previously seemed carved in stone. I think that is the real reason our personal experience stories, the stories we tell about ourselves over and over again, change over time: as our sense of contexts changes so changes our sense of what mattered, what was big and what was little, which words were essential and which words were air.

I told you that this affair taught me how important it is to look at one's own motives, reasons, passions, needs. I'm not sure you can always do this sort of thing alone. I'm certain I could have learned a good deal listening to Jim Bennett—in that conversation we didn't get to have—talking about what he thought I was getting out of our relationship, what strings he was playing and how he knew the harmony. He knows things I don't.

Another thing I learned from thinking about the inquiry I missed because of my anger about the inquiry that wasn't there was this: just because you get burned doesn't mean you've got to shut down. Fire teaches.

And the third thing I learned was said exquisitely by Stéphane Mallarmé more than a century ago in the fourteen lines of *"Don du poème."* At the first breaking of dawn the poet brings to his wife the poem he created in agony in the long night. He tells her that only by the grace of her nurturance can the poem, the "child of the Idumean night," take breath, live.

No story exists out there by itself. The story takes life from two of us: the teller and the listener, writer and reader, actor and watcher, each a necessary participant in the creation of the space in which the utterance takes life, in which all our utterances take life. So this is the good part: all our stories are coauthored and as long as we keep telling them we're never really alone.

NOTES

I want to thank, for their careful reading of and useful comments about earlier versions of this article, Diane Christian, Susan Crofts, Victor A. Doyno, Lydia Fish, Sarah Elder, Roy "Bud" Johns, and Margaret Ratner.

1. Stewart isn't his real name; he preferred not to be identified here. The name "Jim Bennett" is also a pseudonym.

2. See Herr 1977:111–14. Herr situates the Langvei story within his larger description of the Khe Sanh battle (91–178).

In the Valley of the Shadows

(*transAction,* 1971)

For a while in the late 1970s coal prices went up and so did employment in the coalfields of eastern Kentucky, but the subsequent decline in energy prices, coupled with increased mechanization in the mines, undid the gains. In some areas, jobs declined by two-thirds between 1985 and 1991 (Kilborn:1991). When those mining jobs disappeared, so did the jobs of the secondary service workers dependent on those incomes. It's hard times in the mountains once again.

This article happened because Frederic "Fritz" Fleron, an assistant professor at the University of Kentucky, phoned to ask if I'd join him for a visit to Pikeville, a coal-mining town in the eastern part of the state. Buffalo, I told him, was more than five hundred miles from Lexington; surely he had friends closer to hand who could accompany him on the trip. It wasn't company he wanted, Fritz said, it was publicity: community organizers working with the rural poor on the problems of strip mining and labor exploitation were being harassed by local government officials and shot at and blown up by mine owners. He thought an article in a major magazine might do some good.

I had a meeting scheduled only a few days later with Willie Morris, who was then editor of *Harper's Magazine.* I told Willie about Fleron's call. He said it sounded like a good project. I said the piece might run a little long; Willie said that length would not be an issue. He reminded me of Norman

Mailer's piece on the October 1967 antiwar demonstration in Washington, which had occupied the entire February 1968 issue of the magazine.

I called Fleron and told him that Willie had guaranteed a fee, which meant I could afford the trip. "Do you still have that pistol?" was the first thing Fritz asked.

Fritz and I had been graduate students at Indiana University in 1962. There wasn't a great deal to do in Bloomington on weekends, so one day we went to a gun store and acquired instruments of destruction: I bought an enormous and ancient British Webley .44 revolver; Fritz bought a .357 Magnum. We bought boxes of cheap wadcutter reloads from the gun store owner, who thought we were sincere targeteers. We never got it up to tell him that all those rounds went into beer bottles and other litter other people had dumped into the abandoned limestone quarries just outside town.

I told Fritz I no longer had the Webley, I only had the cylinder, which I'd saved when I threw the rest of the pistol away, but I did have a chrome-plated Spanish .380 Llama automatic someone had given me when I'd been doing research on drugs in Texas three years earlier. "But I've never fired it. I don't know if it works," I said.

"Bring it anyway. You have to have *some*thing."

"Why? I'm doing this piece for *Harper's.*"

"The last guy doing this sort of thing in Pikeville, they shot him to death."

I'm sure there was a pause before I said, "Why?"

"He was taking pictures of somebody's house. The owner came out and shot him in the heart."

"What happened?"

"He died."

"I got that. I meant what happened to the guy who shot him."

"Hung jury. Nothing."

I went to Lexington, spent a pleasant evening with Fritz and his wife, LouJean, and early the next morning Fritz and I headed out of the bluegrass country into the hardscrabble mountains. "In the Valley of the Shadows" is about what I saw there.

Curious things happened to it on the way to publication. I sent the manuscript to Willie Morris and didn't hear from him for a long time. I thought of it as at least partially an advocacy piece, one in which the clock mattered. Those people down there were on the line, and it mattered that word of what they were doing and what was happening to them got out while it still might do them some good. I wrote Willie, but got no answer. I phoned him, but he wasn't ever in.

Then an edited manuscript arrived from *Harper's.* It had been cut by about a third. Writers are used to editors who want to make things shorter: writers want space to explore things or to display feathers and editors want to conserve space so they can have as many explorers as possible in the pages at their disposal. But what happened here had nothing to do with ordinary editorial shrinkage or tuning.

The copyedited manuscript I got back had been turned into gibberish. It didn't make journalistic, sociological, or editorial sense. From the marginal notations, I inferred that Midge Decter and two other editors had read the manuscript and someone else had combined the suggestions of all three without noting their mutual incompatibility. I withdrew the article and kept the payment for rent. Willie said he thought that was fair. (I learned later that Willie had nothing to do with the overkill editing: for personal reasons he'd not been around the *Harper's* office during the months I'd been trying to call him, and not long after he resigned the job and went home to Mississippi and began writing again himself.)

I sent the manuscript to Bob Manning, editor of *Atlantic.* Bob said he liked it, but they had just scheduled one of Robert Coles's fine essays on Appalachia and didn't want to run another one on the same geographical area so soon. The tone of the piece wasn't right for the *Times Magazine.* It was now more than a year since I'd mailed the manuscript to *Harper's,* and I guess I lost heart about getting it placed anywhere.

Not long after that, Fleron took a job here in Buffalo. "I was glad that piece never got published," he said when we met on campus one day. I asked him why. "Because you didn't nail those bastards to the wall the way I wanted you to." I told him that nailing them to the wall wouldn't have been very objective or informative or even honest, that things weren't so black and white. "Yes," he said, "but what I wanted was for you to nail them to the wall and you didn't do that." I asked why he'd never told me that, indeed, why he never said anything when I'd shown him a draft of the manuscript. "Didn't matter," he said, which I've never understood.

When I told Diane Christian about the conversation she said, "You should try *transAction* with it." I sent it, along with a dozen photographs, to Irving Louis Horowitz, who accepted the piece almost immediately. Several months later it appeared, but instead of my photos there was one terrific full-page photo by Bruce Davidson and several small photos by Jill Kremetz. The problem was, none were from Pikeville; they were collateral illustrations rather than integral parts of the piece. I called Horowitz in a rage. Why hadn't he told me he was using other people's photographs and why hadn't he used my photographs? He hadn't looked at them, he said.

"What do you mean, you haven't looked at them?"

"Everybody knows writers can't take photographs," he said.

I said a lot of vile things, and he told me to call back whenever I felt up to it.

As I recall, some time after that we had a conversation in which I allowed as I might have been kind of violent in my reaction to his failure to look at the photos, and he allowed as he might have been a little remiss in not looking at the photos. Shortly thereafter I sent him a portfolio of photographs from the Arkansas penitentiary, and Horowitz published them; I think it was the first time *transAction* published photographs that were not illustrating a text. Those photographs were the first publication from a large group of images that would comprise my favorite among my documentary books, *Killing Time: Life in the Arkansas Penitentiary.*

ALONG THE ROADSIDES and in backyards are the cannibalized cadavers of old cars: there is no other place to dump them, there are no junkyards that have any reason to haul them away. Streambeds are littered with old tires, cans, pieces of metal and plastic. On a sunny day the streams and creeks glisten with pretty blue spots from the Maxwell House coffee tins and Royal Crown cola cans. For some reason the paint used by Maxwell House and Royal Crown doesn't wear off very quickly, and while the paint and paper on other cans are peeling to reveal an undistinctive aluminum color, the accumulating blues of those two brands make for a most peculiar local feature.

Winter in eastern Kentucky is not very pretty. In some places you see the gouged hillsides where the strip and auger mines have ripped away tons of dirt and rock to get at the mineral seams underneath; below the gouges you see the littered valleys where the overburden, the earth they have ripped and scooped away, has been dumped in spoil banks. The streams stink from the augerholes' sulfurous exudations; the hillsides no longer hold water back because the few trees and bushes are small and thin, so there is continual erosion varying the ugliness in color only.

Most of the people around here live outside the town in hollers and along the creeks. Things are narrow: the hills rise up closely and flatland is at a premium. A residential area will stretch out for several miles, one or two houses and a road thick, with hills starting up just behind the outhouse. Sometimes, driving along the highway following the Big Sandy River, there is so little flat space that the highway is on one side of the river and the line of houses is on the other, with plank suspension bridges every few miles connecting the two. Everything is crushed together. You may ride five miles without passing a building, then come upon a half-dozen houses, each within ten feet of its neighbor. And churches: the Old Regular Baptist Church, the Freewill Baptist Church, the Meta Baptist Church. On the slopes of the hills are cemeteries, all neatly tended; some are large and old, some have only one or two recent graves in them.

In winter, when the sun never rises very far above the horizon, the valley floors get only about four hours of direct sunlight a day; most of the days are cloudy anyhow. One always moves in shadow, in greyness. Children grow up without ever seeing the sun rise or set.

The day of the company store and company house is gone. So are most of the big companies around here. This is small truck mine country now, and operators of the small mines don't find stores and houses worth their time. The old company houses worth living in have been bought up, either as rental property or for the new owner's personal use; the company houses still standing but not worth living in comprise the county's only public housing for the very poor.

At the end of one of the hollers running off Marrowbone Creek, three miles up a road you couldn't make, even in dry weather, without four-wheel drive, stands an old cabin. It is a log cabin, but there is about it nothing romantic or frontiersy, only grimness. Scratched in the kitchen window, by some unknown adult or child, are the crude letters of the word victory. Over what or whom we don't know. It is unlikely anyway. There are no victories here, only occasional survivors, and if survival is a victory it is a mean and brutal one.

Inside the cabin a Barbie doll stands over a nearly opaque mirror in a room lighted by a single bare 60-watt bulb. In the middle of the room a coal stove spews outrageous amounts of heat. When the stove is empty the room is cold and damp. There is no middle area of comfort. The corrugated cardboard lining the walls doesn't stop drafts very well and most of the outside chinking is gone. On one side of the room with the stove is the entrance to the other bedroom, on the other side is the kitchen. There are no doors inside the house. A woman lives here with her nine children.

If all the nine children were given perfectly balanced full meals three times a day from now on, still some of them would never be well. A 15-year-old daughter loses patches of skin because of an irreversible vitamin deficiency, and sometimes, because of the supporations and congealing, they have to soak her clothing off when she comes home from school. Last month the baby was spitting up blood for a while but that seems to have stopped.

It might be possible to do something for the younger ones, but it is not likely anyone will. The husband went somewhere and didn't come back; that was over a year ago. The welfare inspector came a few months ago and found out that someone had given the family a box of clothes for the winter; the welfare check was cut by $20 a month after that. When the woman has $82 she can get $120 worth of food stamps; if she doesn't have the $82, she gets no food stamps at all. For a year, the entire family had nothing for dinner but one quart of green beans each night. Breakfast was fried flour and coffee. A friend told me the boy said he had had meat at a neighbor's house once.

Bony Hills

This is Pike County, Kentucky. It juts like a chipped arrowhead into the bony hill country of neighboring West Virginia. Pike County has about seventy thousand residents and, the Chamber of Commerce advertises, it produces more coal than any other county in the world. The county seat, Pikeville, has about six thousand residents; it is the only real town for about 30 miles.

The biggest and bitterest event in Pike County's past was sometime in the 1880s when Tolbert McCoy killed Big Ellison Hatfield: it started a feud that resulted in 65 killed, settled nothing and wasn't won by either side. The biggest and bitterest thing in recent years has been the War on Poverty: it doesn't seem to have killed anyone, but it hasn't settled anything or won any major battles either.

About seventy-five hundred men are employed by Pike County's mines: one thousand drive trucks, five hundred work at the tipples (the docks where coal is loaded into railway cars) and mine offices, and six thousand work inside. Most of the mines are small and it doesn't take very many men to work them: an automated truck mine can be handled by about eight men. Some people work at service activities: they pump gas, sell shoes, negotiate contracts (there are about *40* lawyers in this little town), dispense drugs, direct traffic, embalm—all those things that make an American town go. There are six industrial firms in the area; two of them are beverage companies, one is a lumber company; the total employment of the six firms is 122 men and women.

A union mine pays $28–$38 per day, with various benefits, but few of the mines in Pike County are unionized. The truck mines, where almost all the men work, pay $14 per day, with almost no benefits. The United Mine Workers of America were strong here once, but when times got hard the union let a lot of people down and left a lot of bitterness behind. Not only did the union make deals with the larger companies that resulted in many of its own men being thrown out of work (one of those deals recently resulted in a $7.3 million conspiracy judgment against the UMWA and Consolidation Coal Company), but it made the abandonment complete by lifting the unemployed workers' medical cards and shutting down the union hospitals in the area. For most of the area, those cards and hospitals were the only source of medical treatment. There has been talk of organizing the truck mines and someone told me the UMW local was importing an old-time firebreathing organizer to get things going, but it doesn't seem likely the men will put their lives on the line another time.

With Frederic J. Fleron, Jr., an old friend then on the faculty of the University of Kentucky in Lexington, I went to visit Robert Holcomb, president of the Independent Coal Operator's Association, president of the Chamber of Commerce and one of the people in the county most vocally at war with the poverty program. His office door was decorated with several titles: Dixie Mining Co., Roberts Engineering Co., Robert Holcomb and Co., Chloe Gas Co., Big Sandy Coal Co. and Martha Colleries, Inc.

One of the secretaries stared at my beard as if it were a second nose; she soon got control of herself and took us in to see Holcomb. (Someone had said to me the day before, "Man, when Holcomb sees you with that beard on he's gonna be sure you're a communist." "What if I tell him I'm playing Henry the Fifth in a play at the university?" "Then he'll be sure Henry the Fifth is a communist too.") Holcomb took the beard better than the girl had: his expression remained nicely neutral. He offered us coffee and introduced us to his partner, a Mr. Roberts, who sat in a desk directly opposite him. On the wall behind Roberts' head was a large white flying map of the United States with a brownish smear running over Louisiana, Mississippi and most of Texas; the darkest splotch was directly over New Orleans. The phone rang and Roberts took the call; he tilted back in his chair, his head against New Orleans and Lake Pontchartrain.

Holcomb was happy to talk about his objections to the poverty program. "I'm a firm believer that you don't help a man by giving him bread unless you give him hope for the future, and poverty programs have given them bread only." The problem with the Appalachian Volunteers (an antipoverty organization partially funded by OEO, now pretty much defunct) was "they got no supervision. They brought a bunch of young people in, turned 'em loose and said, 'Do your thing.'... I think they have created a disservice rather than a service by creating a lot of disillusionment by making people expect things that just can't happen."

Expanding and Wrecking

He told us something about what was happening. The coal industry had been expanding rapidly. "Over the last eight years the truck mining industry has created an average of 500 new jobs a year." He sat back. "We're working to bring the things in here that will relieve the poverty permanently." He talked of bringing other kinds of industry to the area and told us about the incentives they were offering companies that were willing to relocate. "We know a lot of our people are not fitted for mining," he said.

(It is not just a matter of being "fitted" of course. There is the problem of those who are wrecked by silicosis and black lung who can do nothing but hope their doctor bills won't go up so much they'll have to pull one of the teenage kids out of school and send him to work, or be so screwed by welfare or social security or the UMW pension managers or the mine operators' disability insurance company that the meager payments that do come into some homes will be stopped.)

The truck mines play an ironic role in the local economy: half the men working in them, according to Holcomb, cannot work in the large mines because of physical disability. The small mines, in effect, not only get the leftover coal seams that aren't fat enough to interest Consol or U.S. Steel or the other big companies in the area, but they also get the men those firms have used up and discarded.

From Holcomb's point of view things are going pretty well in Pike County. In 1960 there were $18 million in deposits in Pikeville's three banks; that has risen to $65 million. There are 700 small mines in the county, many of them operated by former miners. "This is free enterprise at its finest," he said.

The next morning he took us on a trip through the Johns Creek area. As we passed new houses and large trailers he pointed to them as evidence of progress, which they in fact are. In the hollers behind, Fred and I could see the shacks and boxes in which people also live, and those Holcomb passed without a word. I suppose one must select from all the data presenting itself in this world, otherwise living gets awfully complex.

We drove up the hill to a small mine. Holcomb told us that the eight men working there produce 175 tons daily, all of which goes to the DuPont nylon plant in South Carolina.

A man in a shed just outside the mine mouth was switching the heavy industrial batteries on a coal tractor. The miner was coated with coal dust and oil smears. He wore a plastic helmet with a light on it; around his waist was the light's battery pack, like a squashed holster. He moved very fast, whipping the chains off and on and winding the batteries out, pumping the pulley chains up and down. Another mine tractor crashed out of the entrance, its driver inclined at 45 degrees. The tractor is about 24 inches high and the mine roof is only 38 inches high, so the drivers have to tilt all the time or get their heads crushed. Inside, the men work on their knees. The tractor backed the buggy connected to it to the edge of a platform, dumped its load, then clanked back inside.

I went into the mine, lying on my side in the buggy towed by the tractor with the newly charged batteries.

Inside is utter blackness, broken only by the slicing beams of light from the helmets. The beams are neat and pretty, almost like a lucite tube poking here and there; the prettiness goes away when you realize the reason the beam is so brilliant is because of the coal and rock dust in the air, dust a worker is continually inhaling into his lungs. One sees no bodies, just occasional hands interrupting the moving light beams playing on the timbers and working face. Clattering noises and shouts are strangely disembodied and directionless.

Outside, I dust off and we head back towards town in Holcomb's truck.

"The temperature in there is 68 degrees all the time," he says. "You work in air-conditioned comfort all year 'round. Most of these men, after they've been in the mine for awhile, wouldn't work above ground." (I find myself thinking of Senator Murphy of California who in his campaign explained the need for bracero labor: they stoop over better than Anglos do.) The miners, as I said, make $14 a day.

"When you see what's been accomplished here in the last ten years it makes the doings of the AVs and the others seem completely insignificant. And we didn't have outside money." The pitted and gouged road is one-lane and we find ourselves creeping behind a heavily loaded coal truck heading toward one of the tipples up the road. "We think welfare is fine, but it should be a temporary measure, not a permanent one. And any organization that encourages people to get on welfare is a detriment to the community." The truck up front gets out of our way, Holcomb shifts back to two-wheel drive, we pick up speed. "These poverty program people, what they tried to do is latch on to some mountain customs and try to convince people they have come up with something new."

He believes business will help everybody; he believes the poverty program has been bad business. He is enormously sincere. Everyone is enormously sincere down here, or so it seems.

So we drove and looked at the new mines and tipples and Robert Holcomb told us how long each had been there and what its tonnage was and how many people each mine employed and how many mines fed into each tipple. One of his companies, he told us, produced 350,000 tons of coal last year and operated at a profit of 15.7 cents per ton.

Hospital death certificates cite things like pneumonia and heart disease. There is no way of knowing how many of those result from black lung and silicosis. The mine owners say very few; the miners and their families say a great many indeed. A lot of men with coated lungs don't die for a long time, but they may not be good for much else meanwhile. Their lungs won't absorb much oxygen, so they cannot move well or fast or long.

"This is a one-industry area," Holcomb had said, "and if you can't work at that industry you can't work at anything." Right. And most of the residents—men wrinkled or contaminated, widows, children—do not work at anything.

Over 50 percent of the families in Pike County have incomes below $3,000 per year. Like land torn by the strip-mining operations, those people simply stay back in the hollers out of sight and slowly erode.

We talked with an old man who had worked in the mines for 28 years. He told us how he had consumed his life savings and two years' time getting his disabled social security benefits.

"See, I got third-stage silicosis and I've got prostate and gland trouble, stomach troubles, a ruptured disc. Now they say that at the end of this month they're gonna take the state aid medical card away. And that's all I've got; I've got so much wrong with me I can't get no insurance. I've had the card two years and now they say I draw too much social security because of last year's increase in social security benefits and they're gonna have to take my medical card away from me after this month. I don't know what in the hell I'm gonna do. Die, I reckon."

"Yeah, yeah," his wife said from the sink.

"It don't seem right," he said. "I worked like hell, I made good money and I doublebacked. Because I worked a lot and draw more social security than lots of people in the mines where they don't make no money, I don't see where it's right for them not to allow me no medical card."

He opened the refrigerator and showed us some of the various chemicals he takes every day. In a neat stack on the table were the month's medical receipts. He said something about his youth, and I was suddenly stunned to realize he was only 51.

"You know," he said, "sand's worse than black lung. Silicosis. It hardens on the lung and there's no way to get it off. In West Virginia I worked on one of those roof-bolting machines. It's about eight, nine-foot high, sandstone top. Burn the bits up drillin' holes in it. And I'd be there. Dust'd be that thick on your lips. But it's fine stuff in the air, you don't see the stuff that you get in your lungs. It's fine stuff. Then I didn't get no pay for it."

"You got a thousand dollars," his wife said.

"A thousand dollars for the first stage. They paid me first stage and I just didn't want to give up. I kept on workin', and now I got third stage. . . . I just hated to give up, but I wished I had of. One doctor said to me, 'If you keep on you might as well get your shotgun and shoot your brains out, you'd be better off.' I still kept on after he told me that. Then I got so I just couldn't hardly go on. My clothes wouldn't stay on me."

The woman brought coffee to the table. "He draws his disabled social security now," she says, "but if he was to draw for his black lung disease they would cut his social security way down, so he's better off just drawing his social security. There's guys around here they cut below what they was drawing for social security. I don't think that's right."

It is all very neat: the black lung, when a miner can force the company doctors to diagnose it honestly, is paid for by company insurance, but payments are set at a level such that a disabled miner loses most of his social security benefits if he takes the compensation; since the compensation pays less than social security, many miners don't put in their legitimate claims, and the net effect is a government subsidy of the insurance companies and mine owners.

Mary Walton, an Appalachian Volunteer, invited Fred and me to dinner at her place in Pikeville one night during our stay. It turned out Mary and I had been at Harvard at the same time and we talked about that place for a while, which was very strange there between those darkening hills. Three other people were at Mary's apartment: a girl named Barbara, in tight jeans and a white shirt with two buttons open and zippered boots, and two men, both of them connected with the local college. One was working with the Model Cities project, the other worked in the college president's office; one was astoundingly tall, the other was built like a wrestler; they all looked aggressively healthy. Barbara's husband worked for the Council of the Southern Mountains in Berea.

The fellow who looked like a wrestler told me at great length that what was going on in Pikeville wasn't a social or economic attack on the community structure, but rather an attack on the structure of ideas and only now was everyone learning that. I asked him what he meant. He said that the poverty workers had once seen their job as enlightening the masses about how messed up things were. "We were ugly Americans, that's all we were. That's why we weren't effective. But now we've learned that you don't change anything that way, you have to get inside the local community and understand it first and work there."

I thought that was indeed true, but I didn't see what it had to do with the structure of the community's ideas; it had to do only with the arrogance or naïveté of the poverty workers, and that was awfully solipsistic. He hadn't said anything about his clients—just himself, just the way his ideas were challenged, not theirs.

The apartment was curiously out of that world. On the walls were posters and lithos and prints and pictures of healthy human bodies looking delicious. The record racks contained the Stones and *Tim Hardin No. 3* and a lot of Bach. Many of the recent books we'd all read and others one had and the others meant to, and Mary and I talked about them, but there was something relative, even in the pleasantness, as if it were an appositive in the bracketing nastiness out there.

When we got back to the car I took from my jacket pocket the heavy and uncomfortable shiny chrome-plated .380 automatic pistol someone had once given me in San Antonio. I put it on the seat next to Fred's .357 revolver. They looked silly there; real guns always do. But people kept telling us how someone else was going to shoot us, or they recounted the story of how Hugh O'Connor, a Canadian film producer down in the next county the year before to make a movie, was shot in the heart by a man with no liking for outsiders and less for outsiders with cameras, and it did seem awfully easy to be an outsider here.

We went to see Edith Easterling, a lifelong Marrowbone Creek resident, working at that time for the Appalachian Volunteers as director of the Marrowbone Folk School. "The people in the mountains really lives hard," Edith said. "You can come into Pikeville and go to the Chamber of Commerce and they'll say, 'Well, there's really no poor people left there. People are faring good.' Then you can come out here and go to homes and you'd just be surprised how poor these people live, how hard that they live. Kids that's grown to 15 or 16 years old that's never had a mess of fresh milk or meats, things that kids really need. They live on canned cream until they get big enough to go to the table and eat beans and potatoes."

She told us about harassment and red-baiting of the AVs by Robert Holcomb, Harry Eastburn (the Big Sandy Community Action Program director, also funded by OEO, a bitter antagonist of any poverty program not under his political control), and Thomas Ratliff, the commonwealth's attorney (the equivalent of a county prosecutor).

Some of the AVs came from out of state, especially the higher paid office staff and technical specialists, but most of the 14 field workers were local people, like Edith. Since becoming involved with the poverty program Edith has received telephone threats and had some windows shot out. The sheriff refused to send a deputy to investigate. Occasionally she gets anonymous calls; some are threats, some call her "dirty communist." She shrugs those away: "I'm a Republican and who ever seen a communist Republican?"

Changing a Way of Life

The Appalachian Volunteers began in the early 1960s as a group of students from Berea College who busied themselves with needed community band-aid work: they made trips to the mountains to patch up dilapidated schoolhouses, they ran tutorial programs, they collected books for needy schools. The ultimate futility of such work soon became apparent and there was a drift in the AV staff toward projects that might affect the lifestyle of some of the mountain communities. In 1966 the AVs decided to break away from their parent organization, the conservative Council of the Southern Mountains. The new, independent Appalachian Volunteers had no difficulty finding federal funding. During the summers of 1966 and 1967 the organization received large OEO grants to host hundreds of temporary volunteer workers, many of them VISTA and Peace Corps trainees. According to David Walls, who was acting director of the AVs when I talked with him, the organization's mission was to "create effective, economically self-sufficient poor people's organizations that would concern themselves with local issues, such as welfare rights, bridges and roads, water systems and strip mining."

It didn't work, of course it didn't work; the only reason it lasted as long as it did was because so much of the AV staff was composed of outsiders, people who had worked in San Francisco and Boston and New York and Washington, and it took a long time before the naïveté cracked enough for the failure to show through.

The first consequence of creating an organization of the impoverished and unempowered is not the generation of any new source or residence of power, but rather the gathering in one place of a lot of poverty and powerlessness that previously were spread out. In an urban situation, the poor or a minority group may develop or exercise veto power: they can manage an economic boycott, they can refuse to work for certain firms and encourage others to join with them, they can physically block a store entrance. It is only when such efforts create a kind of negative monopoly (a strike line no one will cross or a boycott others will respect) that power is generated. When that negative monopoly cannot be created, there is no power—this is why workers can successfully strike for higher wages but the poor in cities cannot get the police to respect their civil liberties enough to stop beating them up; if everyone refuses to work at a factory, the owner must cooperate or close down, but there is nothing anyone can refuse a policeman that will remove the immediate incentive for illegal police behavior. The poor in the mountains cannot strike—they are unemployable anyway, or at least enough of them are to make specious that kind of action. Even if they were to get something going the UMW would not support them. The poor cannot start an economic boycott: they don't spend enough to hold back enough to threaten any aspect of the mountain coal economy. (There have been a few instances of industrial sabotage—I'll mention them later on—that have been dramatic, but pitifully ineffective.) One of the saddest things about the poor in the mountains is they have nothing to deny anyone. And they don't even have the wild hope some city poor entertain that something may turn up; in the mountains there is nothing to hope for.

Another problem with organizations of the very poor is they do not have much staying power: the individual participants are just too vulnerable. So long as the members can be scared or bought off easily, one cannot hope for such groups to develop solidarity. In Kentucky, where welfare, medical aid, disability pensions and union benefits all have a remarkable quality of coming and going with political whims, that is a real problem. Edith

Easterling described the resulting condition: "These people are scared people, they are scared to death. I can talk to them and I can say, 'You shouldn't be scared, there's nothing to be scared about.' But they're still scared."

"What are they scared of," Fred asked her, "losing their jobs?"

"No. Some of 'em don't even have a job. Most of the people don't have jobs. They live on some kind of pension. They're scared of losing their pension. If it's not that, they're scared someone will take them to court for something. 'If I say something, they're going to take me to court and I don't have a lawyer's fee. I don't have a lawyer, so I'd rather not say nothing.' When you get the people to really start opening up and talking, that's when the county officials attack us every time with something."

Publicity and Revenge

For someone who brings troublesome publicity to the community, there are forms of retaliation far crueler than the mere cutting off of welfare or unemployment benefits. One poverty worker told of an event following a site visit by Robert Kennedy a few years ago: "When Kennedy was down for his hearings one of his advance men got in contact with a friend of ours who had a community organization going. They were very anxious to get some exposure, to get Kennedy involved in it. They took the advance men around to visit some families that were on welfare. He made statements about the terrible conditions the children there in two particular homes had to live under. He wasn't indicting the families, he was just talking about conditions in general. These were picked up by the local press and given quite a bit of notoriety—Kennedy Aide Makes the Scene, that sort of thing. After he left, about three days later, the welfare agency came and took away the children from both of those families and put them in homes. . . . This is the control that is over people's lives."

The group with the potential staying power in the mountains is the middle class, the small landowners. They have concrete things to lose while the poor (save in anomalous atrocities such as the one with the children mentioned above) have nothing to lose, they only have possible access to benefits that someone outside their group may or may not let them get. There is a big difference in the way one fights in the two situations. Something else: it is harder to scare the middle class off, for it has not been conditioned by all those years of humiliating control and dependency.

One Appalachian Volunteer, Joe Mulloy, a 24-year-old Kentuckian, realized this. He and his wife decided to join a fight being waged by a Pike County landowner, Jink Ray, and his neighbors, against a strip-mine operator who was about to remove the surface of Ray's land.

Rights for Pennies

The focus of the fight was the legitimacy of the *broadform* deed, a nineteenth-century instrument with which landowners assigned mineral rights to mining companies, usually for small sums of money (50 cents per acre was common). When these deeds were originally signed no landowner had any thought of signing away all rights to his property—just the underground minerals and whatever few holes the mining company might have to make in the hillside to get at the seams. In the twentieth century the coal companies developed the idea of lifting off all the earth and rock above the coal, rather than digging for it, and since the broadform deed said the miner could use whatever means he saw fit to get the coal out, the Kentucky courts held that the miners' land rights have precedence over the surface owners'—even though that meant complete destruction of a man's land by a mining process the original signer of the deed could not have imagined. The strip miners are legally entitled, on the basis of a contract that might be 90 years old, to come to a man's home and completely bury it in rubble, leaving the owner nothing but the regular real estate tax bill with which he is stuck even though the "real estate" has since been dumped in the next creekbed. First come the bulldozers to do the initial clearing (a song I heard in West Virginia, to the tune of "Swing Low, Sweet Chariot," went: "Roll on, big D-9 dozer, comin' for to bury my home/I'm getting madder as you're gettin' closer, comin' for to bury my home"), then they roll in the massive shovels, some of which grow as large as 18.5 million pounds and can gobble 200 tons of earth and rock a minute and dump it all a city block away. Such a machine is operated by one man riding five stories above the ground.

On June 29, 1967, Jink Ray and some neighbors in Island Creek, a Pike County community, blocked with their bodies bulldozers that were about to start stripping Ray's land. With them were Joe and Karen Mulloy. The people themselves had organized the resistance; the Mulloys were simply helping.

With the strip-mining fight on the mountain, the AVs were for the first time involved in something significant. It was also dangerous: the members of the Island Creek group were challenging not only the basis of the local economy, but the federal government as well: the big mines' biggest customer is the Tennessee Valley Authority, and the Small Business Administration supports many of the smaller mine operators. The poverty program and other federal agencies were moving toward open conflict.

What happened was that the poverty program backed down and the local power structure moved in. Eleven days after Governor Edward Breathitt's August 1 suspension of the strip-mine company's Island Creek permit (the first and only such suspension), Pike County officials arrested the Mulloys for sedition (plotting or advocating the violent overthrow of the government). Arrested with them on the same charge were Alan and Margaret McSurely, field workers for the Southern Conference Educational Fund (SCEF), a Louisville-based civil rights organization. McSurely had been hired as training consultant by the AVs during the spring of 1967, but the real reason he had been hired was to restructure the cumbersome organization. One of the first things he did was get the AVs to allow local people on the board of directors; he was fired in a month and went to work for SCEF; they even arrested Carl Braden (SCEF's executive director) and his wife, Anne. Anne Braden had never been in Pike County in her life; the first time Carl Braden had been there was the day he went to Pikeville to post bail for McSurely on the sedition charge.

In Washington, the response to the arrests was immediate; Sargent Shriver's office announced that AV funds would be cut off; no funds previously granted were taken away, but no new money was appropriated after that.

The Pike County grand jury concluded that "A well-organized and well-financed effort is being made to promote and spread the communistic theory of violent and forceful overthrow of the government of Pike County." The grand jury said also that "Communist organizers have attempted, without success thus far, to promote their beliefs among our school children by infiltrating our local schools with teachers who believe in the violent overthrow of the local government." Organizers were "planning to infiltrate local churches and labor unions in order to cause dissension and to promote their purposes." And, finally, "Communist organizers are attempting to form community unions with the eventual purpose of organizing armed groups to be known as 'Red Guards' and through which the forceful overthrow of the local government would be accomplished."

Untouchable Volunteers

The AVs came unglued. The Mulloys became pariahs within the organization. "We spent that whole summer and no AV came to see us at all in Pike County," Joe Mulloy said. "Once they came up to shit on us, but that was the only time. Then the thing of our getting arrested for sedition was what just really flipped everybody.... This was a real situation that you had to deal with, it wasn't something in your mind or some ideological thing. It was real. Another person was under arrest. I think that the feeling of a number of people on the staff was it was my fault that I had been arrested because I had been reckless in my organizing, that I had been on the mountain with the fellas and had risked as much as they were risking and I deserved what I got, and that I should be fired so the program would go on; that I was now a detriment."

That fall, a special three-judge federal court ruled the Kentucky sedition law unconstitutional so all charges against the Mulloys, the Bradens and the McSurelys were wiped out. But the AVs were still nervous. "After the arrests were cleared away," Mulloy said, "things started to happen to me on the staff. I was given another assignment. I was told that I couldn't be a field man any more because I was a public figure identified with sedition and hence people would feel uneasy talking to me, and that I should do research. My truck was taken away and I was given an old car, and I was given a title of researcher rather than field man. It took away considerable voice that I had in the staff until then."

Karen Mulloy said she and Joe really had no choice. "If we had organized those people up there, with possible death as the end result for some of them—fortunately it was kept nonviolent—and if we weren't with them they wouldn't have spoken to us. We took as much risk as they did. We said to them, 'We're not going to organize something for you that we won't risk our necks for either.' An organizer can't do that."

"These people have gone through the whole union experience and that has sold them out," Joe said. "And a great number of people have gone through the poverty war experience and that hasn't answered anybody's problems, anybody's questions. Getting together on the strip-mining issue—if there was ever one issue that the poverty war got on that was good, that was it. It all fell through because when we started getting counterattacked by the operators the poverty war backed up because their funds were being jeopardized. The whole strip-mining issue as an organized effort has collapsed right now and the only thing that's going on is individual sabotage. There's a lot of mining equipment being blown up every month or so, about a million dollars at a time. These are individual or small group acts or retaliation, but the organized effort has ceased."

(Later, I talked with Rick Diehl, the AV research director, about the sabotage. He described two recent operations, both of them very sophisticated, involving groups of multiple charges set off simultaneously. The sheriff didn't even look for the dynamiters: he probably wouldn't have caught them and even if he had he wouldn't have gotten a jury to convict. "And that kind of stuff goes on to some degree all the time," Diehl said. "There's a growing feeling that destroying property is going to shut down the system in Appalachia. The people don't benefit from the coal companies at all, 'cause even the deep mines don't have enough employees. The average number of employees in a deep mine is 16 people. So, you can see, there is nothing to lose. It's that same desperation kind of thing that grips people in Detroit and Watts.")

Organizing Outrage

Even though the sedition charges were dropped, the Mulloys and McSurelys weren't to escape punishment for their organizing outrages.

One Friday the 13th Al McSurely came home late from a two or three day trip out of town, talked with his wife a little while, then went to bed. Margaret went to bed a short time later. "I wasn't asleep at all," she said, "but he was so tired he went right to sleep. I heard this car speed up. Well, I had got into the habit of listening to cars at night, just because we always expected something like this to happen. And sure enough, it did. There was this blast. The car took off and there was this huge blast, and glass and dirt and grit were in my mouth and eyes and hair, and the baby was screaming. So I put on my bathrobe and ran across the street with the baby."

"The state trooper was pretty good," Alan said. "He gave me a lecture: 'The next time this happens call the city police first so they can seal off the holler. They can get here much faster than I can.' I said, 'I'll try and remember that.' "

Joe Mulloy was the only AV with a Kentucky draft board; he was also the only AV to lose his occupational deferment and have his 2-A changed to 1-A. Mulloy asked the board (in Louisville, the same as Muhammed Ali's) for a rehearing on the grounds of conscientious objection, and he presented as part of his evidence a letter from Thomas Merton saying he was Mulloy's spiritual adviser (the two used to meet for talks in Merton's cabin in the woods) and could testify to the truthfulness of Mulloy's C.O. claim. The board refused to reopen the case because, they said, there was no new evidence of any relevance or value. In April 1968 Mulloy was sentenced to five years in prison and a $10,000 fine for refusing induction.

He was fired immediately by the Appalachian Volunteers. Some wanted him out because they honestly thought his draft case would be a major obstacle to his effectiveness with the oddly patriotic mountain people. (In the mountains you can be against the war, many people are, but if your country calls you, you go. It would be unpatriotic not to go. The government and the country are two quite independent entities. The government might screw up the poverty program, run that bad war, work in conjunction with the mine owners and politicians, but it isn't the government that is calling you—it is the country. Only a weirdo would refuse that call. But once you're in you are working for the government, and then it is all right to desert.) Others on the AV staff objected to Mulloy's getting involved in issues that riled up the authorities. The staff vote to get rid of him was 20 to 19.

What the AVs failed to admit was that the changing of Mulloy's draft status was an attack on them as well: the only reason for the change was the strip-mine fight. The draft board had joined the OEO, the TVA, the mine owners, the political structure of the state and the UMW in opposition to effective organization of the poor in the mountains.

I asked Joe how he felt about it all now. "I don't know if I can really talk about this objectively," he said. "I feel in my guts as a Kentuckian a great deal of resentment against a lot of these people. And some of them are my friends that have come in and stirred things up and then have left. The going is really tough right now. I'm still here, all the people that have to make a living out in those counties are still there with their black lung. I don't think anything was accomplished. It's one of those things that's going to go down in history as a cruel joke: the poverty war in the mountains."

The two bad guys of the story, I suppose, should be Robert Holcomb, spokesman for the mine owners in the county, and commonwealth's attorney Thomas Ratliff, the man who handled the prosecution in the sedition and who was (coincidentally, he insists) Republican candidate for lieutenant governor at the time; Ratliff got rich in the mine business, but is now into a lot of other things. Like most bad guy labels, I suspect these are too easy. I'll come back to that.

I rather liked Ratliff even though there were things I knew about him I didn't like at all. It is quite possible he really does believe, as he said he does, that the McSurelys and the Bradens are communist provocateurs; there are people in America who believe such menaces exist, though not very many of them are as intelligent as Ratliff.

He claims the defendants in the sedition case had "a new angle on revolution—to do it locally and then bring all the local revolutions together and then you got a big revolution. Now whether it would have succeeded or not I don't know. I think it possibly could have, had they been able to continue to get money from the Jolly Green Giant, as they call Uncle Sam. I certainly think with enough money, and knowing the history of this area, it was not impossible."

What seems to have bothered him most was not the politics involved but the bad sportsmanship: "The thing that rankled me in this case, and it still does, this is really what disturbed me more about this thing than anything else, was the fact that . . . they were able to use federal money . . . to promote this thing. Frankly, I would be almost as opposed to either the Republican party or the Democratic party being financed by the federal money to prevail, much less a group who were avowed communists, made no bones about it that I could tell, whose objective was revolution, the forceful and violent overthrow of the local government and hopefully to overthrow the federal government, and it was being financed by federal tax money!"

Once Ratliff got off his communist menace line, I found myself agreeing with him as much as I had with some of the remarks Joe Mulloy had made.

Ratliff spoke eloquently on the need for a negative income tax, for massive increases on the taxes on the mine operators, things like that. (Whether he meant the things he said is impossible to tell; one never knows with politicians, or anyone else for that matter.)

"It's the reaction to this sort of situation that really bothers me," he said, "because—there is no question about it—there is some containment of free speech, free expression, when you get a situation like this. People become overexcited and overdisturbed. And the laws of physics play in these things: for every action there's a reaction, and the reaction, unfortunately, is often too much in this kind of situation. You begin seeing a communist behind every tree. That's bad. Because there isn't a communist behind every tree, or anything like that.

"But I think they've accomplished one thing, not what they thought they would.... That's the tragic part of it, I don't think they've uplifted anybody. I think they have left a lot of people disappointed, frustrated.... But I think they have scared the so-called affluent society into doing something about it. Maybe. I think there are people more conscious of it because of that."

It is so easy to write off Holcomb or Ratliff as evil men, grasping and groping for whatever they can get and destroying whatever gets in the way; for a poverty worker it is probably necessary to think such thoughts, that may be the mental bracing one needs to deal as an opponent.

But I think it is wrong.

Holcomb is an ex-miner who made it; uneducated and not particularly smart, he somehow grooved on the leavings in that weird economy and got rich. He thinks what he did is something anyone ought to be able to do: it is the American dream, after all. His failure is mainly one of vision, a social myopia hardly rare in this country. From Holcomb's point of view, those people stirring up the poor probably are communist agitators—why else would anyone interfere with the "free enterprise system at its best"? If you tried to tell him that a system that leads to great big rich houses on one side of town and squalid leaky shacks on the other might not be the best thing in this world he'd think you were crazy or a communist (both, actually) too. And Thomas Ratliff is hardly the simple Machiavelli the usual scenario would demand.

Picking out individuals and saying the evil rests with them is like patching schoolhouses and expecting the cycle of poverty to be broken. Even when you're right you're irrelevant. What is evil in the mountains is the complex of systems, a complex that has no use or place or tolerance for the old, the wrecked, the incompetent, the extra, and consigns them to the same gullies and hollers and ditches as the useless cars and empty Maxwell House coffee tins and Royal Crown cola cans, with the same lack of hate or love.

The enemies of the poverty program, malicious or natural, individual or collective, turn out to be far more successful than they could have hoped or expected. One reason for that success is the cooperation of the victims: groups like the AVs become, as one of their long-time members said, "top-heavy and bureaucratic, a bit central office bound. We are . . . worried about maintaining the AV structure, and responding to pressures from foundations and OEO, rather than from community people." The federal government, presumably the opponent of poverty here, plays both sides of the fence: it supports activities like the AVs (so long as they are undisturbing), but it also supports the local Community Action Program, which is middle-class dominated and politically controlled; it created a generation of hustlers among the poor who find out that only by lying and finagling can they get the welfare and social security benefits they legitimately deserve; it strengthens the local courthouse power structures by putting federal job programs in control of the county machines and by putting the Small Business Administration at its disposal; it commissions studies to document the ill effects of strip mining and simultaneously acts, through TVA, as the largest consumer of the product.

The mood is much like the McCarthy days of the early 1950s: actual legal sanctions are applied to very few people, but so many others are smeared that other people are afraid of contagion, of contamination, even though they know there is nothing to catch. They avoid issues that might threaten some agency or person of power, they stop making trouble, stop looking for trouble, they keep busy, or they stay home—and no one ever really says, when faced by the complex, "I'm scared."

Everyone has something to do: busy, busy, busy. I remember a visit to the AV office in Prestonsburg; they had there what must have been one of the largest Xerox machines in the state of Kentucky; it was used for copying newspaper articles; someone on the staff ran it. There was an AV magazine assembled by a staff member who, if some of the foundations grants had come through, would have gotten a full-time assistant. The mining went on; the acting director of the AVs, Dave Walls, went about hustling private foundations grants and being sociable and vague and disarming to visitors, and not much of anything really happened.

I visited eastern Kentucky again a short time ago. There were some changes. The weather was softer and some leaves were on the trees, so you couldn't see the shacks back in the hollers unless you drove up close; you couldn't see the hillside cemeteries and junkyards at all.

I found out that Governor Louis Nunn had blocked any new AV funds and most of the other money had gone, so there were ugly battles over the leavings, mixed with uglier battles over old political differences within the organization itself.

Edith Easterling was fired; she now has a Ford grant to travel about the country and look at organizing projects. Rick Diehl has gone somewhere else. Mary Walton is now a staff reporter for the Charleston (W.Va.) *Gazette*. The Prestonsburg AV office is still open—with a small group of lawyers working on welfare rights problems; that is the only AV activity still alive and no one knows how much longer there will be any money for that.

I ran into Dave Walls in a movie house in Charleston. The show was *Wild River* with Montgomery Clift and Lee Remick, and it was about how good TVA is and what a swell guy Montgomery Clift is and how homey and true a mountain girl Lee Remick is. Anyway, I saw Dave there and we talked a moment during intermission. He still draws a subsistence salary from the AVs, still lives in Berea, over in the Bluegrass country far and nicely away from it all. He is going to school at the University of Kentucky in Lexington, doing graduate work in something. He looked just the same, no more or less mild. Someone asked him, "What's going on in the mountains now? What happened to everything?" He shrugged and smiled, "I don't know," he said. "I haven't gone to the mountains in a long time."

Well, for the other people, the ones who were there before, things are pretty much the same. That woman and her nine children still live in that shack in Poorbottom. The man who worked the mines for 28 years is still kept marginally alive by the chemical array in his refrigerator he still somehow manages to afford.

A Distrust of Strangers

I met Jink Ray, the man who faced down the bulldozers, on that recent trip. When we drove up he had just put out some bad honey and the bees were a thick swarm in the front of the house. We went into a sitting room-bedroom where his wife sat before an open coal fire and each wall had one or two Christs upon it. We talked about the strip-mine fight. On one wall was a photo of him with Governor Breathitt the day the governor came up to stop the strippers. We went outside and talked some more, standing by the overripe browning corn standing next to a patch of corn just about ripe, the hills thickly coated and overlapping to form a lush box canyon behind him. He pointed to the hillside the other side of the road and told us they'd been augering up there. "You can't see it from down here this time of year, but it's bad up there." The seepage killed the small streams down below: nothing lives in those streams anymore. "We used to get bait in them streams, nothing now, and fish used to grow there before they went to the river. Not now." Suddenly his face hardened, "Why you fellas asking me these questions?" We told him again that we were writing about what had happened in Pike County. "No," he said, "that ain't what you are. I believe you fellas are here because you want to get stripping going again, you want to know if I'll back off this time." He talked from a place far behind the cold blue eyes that was just so awful. We protested, saying we really were writers, but it didn't work–it's like denying you're an undercover agent or homosexual, there's no way in the world to do it once the assumption gets made, however wrong. He talked in postured and rhetorical bursts awhile and it seemed a long time until we could leave without seeming to have been run off. Leaving him standing there looking at the yellow Hertz car backing out his driveway, his face still cold and hard, polite to the end, but . . . But what? Not hating, but knowing: he knows about strangers now, he knows they are there to take something away, to betray, to hustle, he knows even the friendly strangers will eventually go back wherever strangers go when they are through doing whatever they have come down to do, and he will be just where he is, trying with whatever meagre resources he's got to hold on to the small parcel of land he scuffled so hard to be able to own. He'll not trust anyone again, and for me that was perhaps the most painful symptom of the failure and defeat of the poverty program in the mountains.

The others: Joe Mulloy, after about two years in the courts, finally won the draft appeal he should never have had to make in the first place; Al and Margaret McSurely were sentenced to prison terms for contempt of Congress after they refused to turn over their personal papers to a Senate committee investigating subversion in the rural South. Tom Ratliff is still commonwealth's attorney, there in the county of Pike, in the state of Kentucky. And Robert Holcomb still has his mines, his colleries, his offices, and his fine and unshaken belief in the American Way.

The Battle of the Pentagon

(*Atlantic Monthly,* 1968)

Newspaper coverage of the October 1967 peace demonstration in Washington, D.C., was almost uniformly hostile. Instead of focusing on the wide range of interests represented on the Mall and at the Pentagon, the press focused on a small number of hardly representative incidents and individuals, and even then the reportage wasn't particularly accurate. It would be another year before the daily press began getting in tune with the shifting mood of the nation and would write about antiwar demonstrators without a shield of pejorative adjectives. The magazine press was far kinder to the Movement. *Atlantic* published this piece in its January 1968 issue, and the following month *Harper's* devoted its entire issue to Norman Mailer's description of the early part of the march and his arrest (that account was subsequently published in book form as *The Armies of the Night*).

Jimmy Breslin's piece (quoted at length in the article) could have been written by Johnson administration flacks, and perhaps it was. Looking back on this event I'm struck by how many of those wanting to minimize the significance or legitimacy of the march dismissed the participants by mere name-calling. "Hippies" seems to have been the favorite epithet. Epithets, as any student of the Hitlertime knows, are a necessary ingredient when you're on the morally untenable side of an ethical issue. It's an old trial lawyer's gambit: if you don't have the facts, smear the witness.

I was wrong when I wrote in this article that the October 1967 antiwar demonstration at the Pentagon was "not a continuation nor a degeneration of the civil rights movement; it is something quite different." The antiwar activists took most of their best techniques from the civil rights struggle, and many of the same people served in both campaigns.

And my comments about the limits of governmental mendacity in the final paragraph turn out to have been naive. Revelations in the 1970s about the FBI's COINTELPRO operation proved that the federal agents were not only snooping around in the civil rights and antiwar movements but had fielded paid agitators in both movements; these agents were specifically assigned the job of encouraging people to engage in activities that might lead them to violate the law. COINTELPRO's paid informants in defense organizations funneled information about legal defense strategy to federal prosecutors. It was grimy stuff and remains one of the reasons hardly anyone in the FBI refers to FBI headquarters by its official name: the John Edgar Hoover Building.

IN NONE OF THE ACCOUNTS I've so far read of the October 21 and 22 peace demonstration in Washington do I discover any sense of what that weekend really *meant.* The older reporters, who were behind the soldiers' lines or on the Pentagon roof or inside the temporary war room, wrote about hippies and Maoists; the kids, on the other side of the line, wrote about the awful brutality of the U.S. marshals. Each wrote with enough half-truth to feel justified in excluding the other; neither moved beyond the immediate lure of invective and self-righteousness to ask what that awful weekend tells us about our American land in this darkening year.

I was there; I suppose I can't claim absolute objectivity either. To qualify my point of view, I'll first tell you something of what I did and saw that Saturday afternoon and evening and in the early hours of Sunday morning.

"I just love them flower girls," a man in his thirties said to me, staring at one pretty woman in a very short skirt, "but I wish there was more of them."

He was right: there weren't very many. Hippies were there, but so was everyone else. The crowd was an American pastiche: older people with graying hair and grim faces, quite at home among the more numerous youngsters of college age; some children, playing among the placards; people in the middle—like myself at thirty-one—not quite knowing whether to be juniors in the mature section or graybeards in the young. Many of the people were political, involved in political activity as part of a modus vivendi, but not most.

From atop the Lincoln Memorial policemen peered at the city and at us through field glasses; one had a camera with about a 300-millimeter telephoto lens. Down below, half the people seemed to carry cameras. It was like the start of a love-in, or perhaps midafternoon at a county fair. From time to time, early in the afternoon, the loudspeaker called for the lost, gave locations of groups, requested that people gather at their respective staging areas. There were signs, most of them direct and simple:

END THE WAR

SUPPORT OUR BOYS IN VIETNAM: BRING THEM HOME

NO MORE NAPALM

HELL NO, WE WON'T GO.

Others were more imaginative or aggressive:

PULL OUT LIKE LBJ'S FATHER SHOULD HAVE

PROVE YOU'RE A MAN: MAKE LOVE NOT WAR (this one toted by a girl with whom that prospect was not unattractive).

There was a pleased roar from the crowd: veterans of the Lincoln Brigade arrived with a sign that read, "No More Guernicas."

At the reflecting pool between the Washington Monument and the Lincoln Memorial people were grouping below and around large lettered signs. The C contingent in the parade order was the veterans. I was undecided whether to march with them, with former students and friends gathering about a Harvard banner, or with current students and friends around a Buffalo sign. The veterans' contingent should be as large as possible, I decided, so at first I went there. As I walked by, a man tried to sell me the veterans' organization's official cap. "I don't want a cap," I said. I thought the caps were silly.

"But you got to have a cap. Man, the mass media see us with all those caps, it'll get all kinds of coverage." I told him again that I did not want a cap. "But if you don't have a cap, it don't mean a thing. Your marching here just don't mean a thing. Might as well not be here. Two bucks, Mac, that's all." I gave two dollars to someone collecting for the Mobilization Committee and joined the students elsewhere.

Robert Lowell introduced me to Norman Mailer, whom I had never met before. He was smaller than I'd thought and quite dapper in a dark blue suit; he looked rather like a healthy pimp. Contrary to *Time* magazine's report, Mailer was neither drunk nor incoherent. He was one of the first people arrested at the Pentagon, and therefore had to miss the most interesting parts of the day's events, but it wasn't because he didn't know what he was doing; posturing was very difficult when you came right up to the soldiers and marshals: their clubs were large, and they were using them nastily.

I wandered around the pool, taking photographs. I have one photograph of two old men sitting on a park bench near the end of the reflecting pool; they are obviously regular residents and are quite amused at the parade. Near them: a woman pushes a baby carriage by a boy with a flower in his lapel; another youth in dark suit and tie carries a light raincoat; another carries a poster. In the next frame, taken about a minute later, one of the two old men is poking in a trash barrel, looking for food, while his friend continues to watch the crowd; on their left stands a man in a very dark suit, with very dark tie, very dark glasses, very white shirt, and very bald head; a cop, FeeBie, CIA, something like that.

A chant from somewhere:

Hey, hey, LBJ
How many kids did you kill today?

And then another: "What do you want?" yells a single voice. "Peace," call back a dozen voices. "When do you want it?" "Now!" The call and response continue until there are several hundred voices responding; the pace quickens until the leader drops out and the crowd chants: *Peace, now! peace, now! peace, now! peace, now! peace, now!*

The action got going on the platform. The Bread and Puppet Theater parodied patriotic hymns, then performed a parable, "The Great Warrior." Three busloads from Oakland, California, arrived—"the real heroes in the fight for peace," said the announcer; the crowd cheered. A flautist fluted. Malcolm X's sister gave a rather simpleminded and incoherent speech about "barbarickisms." There were many speeches, but hardly anyone could hear them. It didn't matter much: they weren't for the crowd anyway; they were for the TV cameramen and wire services, whose electronic rigs were arrayed in a brilliant display of technology in the sun. Phil Ochs warbled a song declaring the war over, and Peter, Paul, and Mary sang about the Great Mandala. The music was the first key that something was wrong: it was surface, anachronistic. Those things belonged back in 1963, but not now. If anything, the main stage should have had something violent and angry, the Jefferson Airplane, or even the Fugs, who were elsewhere.

Everything went late: moving out took too long; the bridge across the Potomac was too narrow for the crowds; a new fence confused the first marchers and delayed those behind; people were tired and hungry and thirsty before they ever reached the Pentagon grounds.

It was obvious that the Buffalo contingent wouldn't move for some time, so I went forward and joined the group ambiguously identified as "Professionals." For a while I walked with some white-coated doctors and nurses from a New York hospital, but the lines mixed crossing a road, and I was between some college students from Long Island and high school kids from Detroit. The lines went and stopped, went and stopped; I moved out and walked along the bridge's sidewalk. Helicopters buzzed constantly, filled with newsmen taking our pictures, or FBI doing the same.

The area for the Pentagon demonstration was a large triangular grassy place in front of the Mall, but the new eight-foot fence blocked off the area. At the Pentagon North parking lot there seemed now nowhere to go but back; people milled around without design. I talked with a few older people who said they were going to walk to D.C. for dinner, then would join their buses later. Hundreds were walking back toward the Lincoln Memorial.

I decided to walk to National Airport. I strolled around the Pentagon grounds. At one point I skirted some MP's who didn't seem to be guarding anything in particular and found a break in the fence. I walked through it, climbed a hill, passed through a small grove of trees, and found, quite by accident, several thousand people in front of the Mall. It was like stumbling upon the Hollywood Bowl. I never did make my plane. More and more people found that hole in the fence, and by late afternoon the fence was trampled to the ground.

On the lawn triangle, a man with a bullhorn stood on the edge of the parapet and told us what was happening on the elevated parking lot which forms the Pentagon's main entrance. Once he yelled for a doctor: someone had fallen off the wall and broken a leg. He gave reports of clubbings. Then he said, "They've surrounded Dr. Spock. Ten MP's have surrounded him. And more are around them. The MP's have him trapped."

When I saw the Buffalo sign and wandered over to see if any of my students were there, I met two other professors from my department, and one said, "Let's walk near the wall." We did, intending nothing but a look around from below. Occasionally someone scurried up the ropes dangling from the parapet at the left side of the Mall. The climb ranged from about ten to sixteen feet, depending where you stood on the row of steps that ran parallel to the parapet. Bob and Al went up the rope and disappeared over the parapet.

I never *could* climb a rope, but I managed to get to the top. The first thing I saw was a sea of helmets that resolved themselves into a row of soldiers with their rifles at the port backed by another row with their rifles at parade rest; behind them about one hundred and fifty soldiers in five ranks covered the main steps. The second thing I saw was a woman about sixty years old who carried a coat that looked like mine. "This is your coat, I think," she said, handing it to me. Where she got it, I don't know.

Bob came over and said, "Man, you just had to come up here."

"Why?"

"I've got your camera, and I don't want to be holding it when it gets busted."

I thanked him and took it, so I could be holding it when it got busted. The logic seemed logical.

A girl of about twenty walked by with a cookie in each hand. I stared at them, mostly because they were so incongruous with the rifles and shiny helmets in the background. "Want one?" she said.

I did, but I said, "No, you only have two."

"It's OK," she said. "I had another one a little while ago. Somebody gave me three."

She went away. Far above, on the roof, were soldiers with rifles and, someone said, automatic weapons. There was also a TV camera, which I later learned was the main reason more of us were not attacked on the Mall. It wasn't until after the last camera crew left that night, about ten thirty, someone said, that the brutality got bad there; it was bad elsewhere all evening, however.

A boy in a suit was distributing small wet rags from a large plastic bag. "For the tear gas."

A Negro gave me a Wash-and-Dri. "Use this first," he said, "It's better." I must have looked dubious, because he said, "It really is, man; I've tried them both, and I know."

A sergeant tightened the front line, moving the men shoulder to shoulder; whenever there was room enough he introduced a new soldier; he adjusted until the line was solid. Hovering everywhere were the marshals. The soldiers were poised, as if we were going to attack.

Down below, some kids put flowers in the muzzles of the MP's rifles. The MP's were under orders not to move, so they didn't know what to do. Some of them shook the flowers out. One smiled. Another remained motionless. The sergeant came by, and said, "Jones, get that fucking flower out of your muzzle." Jones did.

About this time reality and the press diverge most acutely. Jimmy Breslin (Washington *Post,* October 22) wrote that an Airborne captain told his men, "A Company, hold your ground. A Company. Nobody comes and nobody goes. Just hold your ground A Company." Breslin, who heard the order locking the demonstrators in, was appalled that kids later used the side of the Pentagon as a toilet target. There were of course no toilets on the Mall, but Breslin, secure and warm, didn't understand that—the comfortable never understand the difference between the necessary and the gratuitous. Breslin's biological imperception wasn't nearly so gross as his visual distortions. "These were not the kind of kids who were funny," he wrote. "These were the small core of dropouts and drifters and rabble who came to the front of what had started out as a beautiful day, one that would have had meaning to it. They turned a demonstration for peace, these drifters in raggedy clothes, into a sickening, club-swinging mess. At the end of the day, the only concern anybody could have was for the soldiers who were taking the abuse."

Breslin may have been there, but he wrote as if he hadn't. Had he been out with the crowd, he would have known that hardly anyone was raggedy; had he been curious later, all he had to do was examine the photographs accompanying his own copy in the *Post.* Drifters? Was he taking employment statistics? And what on earth does he mean about "beautiful" and "meaning": that we should have spent the day at the Lincoln Memorial listening to Peter, Paul, and Mary singing about the Great Mandala? that no one should be angry about anything? that it should be a sunny afternoon on the grass after which everyone goes home feeling ratified and discharged, like any good old-fashioned liberal who has talked out his need to act?

Breslin, I should point out, is the only reporter I've read who seemed to believe the Department of Defense claim that the demonstrators threw the tear gas at themselves to get sympathy. Other reporters, who *saw* soldiers throwing the canisters, suggested that the department was either confused or mendacious.

I did not *see* troopers fire tear gas. I did see troopers remove their helmets, fix their gas masks by the numbers, replace their helmets, and resume their port arms positions while their sergeant aimed his gas launcher and a bunch of people who had been quietly standing on the grass ran like hell. A few minutes later something made my eyes runny and me sneezy.

James Reston wrote that about this time "the event was taken over by the militant minority.... It is difficult to report publicly the ugly and vulgar provocation of many of the militants. They spat on some of the soldiers in the front line at the Pentagon and goaded them with the most vicious personal slander" (*Times,* October 23).

It is true that some of the militants were militant; that's why we call them militants. What Reston doesn't say is how small a portion of the population at the Pentagon they were. As an indication, as the *New Republic* pointed out, all those thousands of people broke just *one* window. I knew many of the people up on the front Mall, and hardly any of them were particularly political or militant. Some people cursed at the soldiers; most just looked at them; some chatted or smiled or lectured. The MP's in the line didn't earn the loathing earned by the marshals and paratroopers, and many of the kids assumed the MP's were draftees there against their will. (We met one boy with bruises who defended the soldiers: "They're wrong, but they're under orders. What can they do? A lot would like to join us."

"How do you know?"

"Hell, man, I'm in the service myself. Just have a weekend liberty.")

The Pentagon show was not Maoist, it was not SDS, it was not any organization's affair. They were all there, surely, but so were others of us, "traditional pacifists," as Reston said, "like the earnest young professors who dislike the War because it seems to them a senseless war, a war without honest purpose, a war that belies their idea of America and gives the lie to the idealistic language that is used by the President and Secretary of State to defend it. Also they feel its terrible human misery, the unfairness of asking young men who are not professional soldiers to die in this cause." And even more, I think, the unfairness of asking the people of Vietnam to submit to gradual attenuation so that the United States can conduct this exercise.

You saw a lot of things outside the Pentagon if you looked around. I saw a marshal reach over the line down below with a club and swipe any head in reach. The soldiers grabbed someone on the parapet and began beating him and beating him and beating him. The crowd booed and roared and began throwing things at the MP's. Someone screamed at them, "Maintain nonviolence! Violence is their bag, not ours." They settled down and stopped throwing things, and after a while the MP's stopped beating the boy.

A soldier collapsed on the stairs, one of my students told me. One demonstrator tried to keep the soldier from falling, and about five soldiers and a marshall pounced on him. They stopped beating him when the TV spotlights came on. "But I think the soldiers weren't doing it for real; they were just going through the motions because they had to. They were pulling their blows. Otherwise they would have killed that guy, five of them pounding him like that. It was just the marshal who hit hard."

"The marshals didn't pull any punches," another student said. "Man, I saw them reaching through our lines and yank someone out, and they beat him unconscious."

"We were on the line, and I heard a yell that a soldier had taken off his helmet and dropped his rifle and was coming to our side. I turned and I saw him being dragged by the wrists into the Pentagon. You could see he hadn't collapsed or anything like that; they were mad, and he was fighting them."

Someone came over the wall; he carried a green plastic canteen. He offered some of us a drink of water. It was the first I'd had since early that day. The fellow who had brought the canteen took a turn, then passed it around again. When it was empty he went back over the wall, going for more. I later learned that the police wouldn't let cars within a mile of the place, so if you went for food you had to stop on one of the approach roads and unload your food- and water-carrying passengers before the police chased you away and roving bands of soldiers and marshals and Nazis spotted them and took up positions in the woods to jump them as they came through in the dark.

A familiar smell occasionally drifted past. One youth held his grass out to me, and said, "Ain't it the weirdest. Get caught with this, and they can give you five years; drop your napalm bombs good, and they give you a medal."

On the North wall a man walked to two girls sitting on the parapet. "You better move," he said. "Why?" "This is the Pissing Wall." "What?" "You heard of the Wailing Wall in Jerusalem? Well, this is the Pissing Wall in the Pentagon." The girls moved, laughing.

In the deep left corner I saw a flash of flame, and the people over there began a cheer. There was another flame on the parapet, and the mob below let out a pleased yell. Among the thousands of people below there was a sudden rash of small flickering lights in the dark, then a small bonfire. No need to wonder what they were burning.

When the reporters had gone to bed or typewriter, and most of the demonstrators had left in their chartered buses, and the night was cold, the troopers and marshals formed wedges that poked into the front lines of the demonstrators.

"As the advancing line of troops came in contact with the squatting demonstrators," said the New York *Times* news story, "United States marshals arrested the youths—apparently on the technical charge of having crossed official lines—and hauled them away, limp, to waiting vans." It wasn't quite that simple: the limpest were the unconscious. When the soldiers moved through, the marshals came right behind them, clubbing. *And this was while the demonstration permit was still in effect.*

"In a sort of war of attrition," wrote one reporter, "U.S. marshals quietly arrested over-zealous protestors one-by-one most of Sunday morning. Arrests were spaced several minutes apart in an effort to avoid trouble."

"I'll tell you the way it went," one student told me. "About ten P.M. the MP's were relieved by the paratroopers. They started clubbing and beating then. They sometimes hit the girls in the breasts instead of the head. We were sitting close with arms linked. The marshals would wedge and club, the troopers used rifle butts and feet; they clubbed them all the way to the wagons. I remember someone screaming, 'Stop it, stop it! I'm willing to submit to the arrest, just stop beating me!' But they didn't stop." Someone called on the bullhorn for Van Cleve of GSA, who had given the demonstration permit, to explain why the beatings and arrests were going on. They asked for anyone to explain. No one explained, except the troopers and marshals, with boots, clubs, and butts. Sometimes, when the Mall beatings started, the TV lights suddenly flooded the place for filming; immediately the soldiers would pull back. "But they got some footage I know." So far as I know, none of it appeared anywhere.

One boy said to me, "I understand how the Viet Cong holds out now. When those bastards started beating us with those sticks, and we were just *sitting* there, I knew they wouldn't make me give in. They could arrest me and chase me away, but not make me quit. Not now."

Many said it was a miracle the troops did not lose their temper and charge and maul the marchers. That is just the thinking the kids were marching against: someone disagrees with you, someone says something nasty to you, kill the sonofabitch and all his friends, wipe up the territory with his head, *yah yah yah.* No, it is the kids I give the credit to; they did not, for the most part, blow their cool; they did not let the seething fury within them give way to actions they knew would be fatal—not to them; many got beaten anyhow, just for being there—to the fading dream of a nonviolent confrontation that was still somehow meaningful.

Fading fast. All those troops and all those guns were there to save Washington not from some hideous gook-looking furriner, but *them.*

Did you ever suddenly realize that you were something your government needed protection against? Perhaps the first thing you do is laugh at the absurdity, the second is ask yourself why, the third is stop laughing.

Almost every newspaper account emphasized the hippie dress and hair, yet I don't think more than a small fraction of the population there affected that style. Certainly none of the group news photos bears out the notion that it was a hippie affair. The experienced few wore old clothes because they saw no point in having good clothes bloodstained.

The worst troops were the U.S. marshals, who work for the Department of Justice; next were the methodical paratroopers of the 82nd Airborne, who previously distinguished themselves for duty in the Dominican Republic and Detroit. The MP's were pretty good; sometimes when they were beating someone, they obviously weren't doing it with conviction—otherwise the people wouldn't have been alive; the marshals were under no such restraint. (The Washington *Post* published a photo of two marshals beating the hell out of a fallen demonstrator. The caption was "U.S. Marshal threatens fallen youth.")

Though I may be a little eccentric, I am not a hippie, beatnik, Communist, crank, crackpot, or otherwise distinguishable weirdo. Few of the people on the Pentagon Mall were hippies, beatniks, cranks, crackpots, or otherwise distinguishable weirdos. It was just demonstrators, journalists, marshals, and soldiers; only the last two were in uniform and responsible to a central command.

About 3 A.M. in a gas station on the east side of Washington we met a twenty-year-old Negro student from Columbia who was looking for a ride. He was lost, he said; someone had picked him up on the highway outside the Pentagon and dropped him off here. We asked him what had happened.

He had been on the right side of the Mall. The troops started advancing, kicking the people sitting there, then arresting and beating those whose positions they passed (for having crossed their lines). A white boy with him said, "That's the truth," and showed us a large bruise on the side of his face.

The Negro boy said someone stepped on him, and when he scrambled out of the way, he was beaten and arrested for resisting arrest. "I didn't understand it either," he said. When they took him inside the building, someone hit him again, and he had an asthma attack. The marshals panicked and after having a doctor give him a shot of adrenalin, which brought him out of the spasm, they decided not to arrest him. "They had some kind of rule that you had to have your picture taken with the marshal or soldier that arrested you. A girl was unconscious on the floor with a big bandage on her head, blood leaking through. The marshal lay down on the floor next to her, and they took their picture. But they said they couldn't find my marshal, so they told me to get out. I was going to go get arrested again—they arrested all my friends—but they threw me in a car and took me up to that highway and pushed me out, and said, 'Don't come back.' And they drove away." Their reason was obvious: to have a bruised Negro student die in captivity would be too much; no one would believe the asthma story. The boy was worried that he wasn't with his friends: "I'm broke. At least they get hot food and a place to sleep tonight." We gave him some money, and he went off.

What did it all accomplish? The next day, and during the next week, the Johnson Administration sent the greatest air armadas yet to bomb downtown Haiphong and Hanoi. That showed us good. Can't mess with Johnson; he won't be pushed around by a bunch of yellowniggerlovingjewradicaldopefiendcommiesympfaggotpeacebeatnikhippies. He'll prove he's right if he has to blow Vietnam to the four winds. So we didn't stroke his conscience any, we merely piqued his ego.

Sunday morning, Johnson went to church, and the pastor of the National City Christian Church stroked his President's ego with a Christian denunciation of the demonstration: "There are those in this nation who do not deserve to be free and to play fast and loose with that freedom.

"What do they know, these bearded oafs who listen to the strumming of lugubrious guitars? To be loved is not the end of greatness."

I don't understand the non sequitur, nor do I understand whom he was talking about: I didn't see any oafs, and I didn't hear any lugubrious guitars. Love, I'll agree, is not the end of Johnson's greatness. Oafs—those kids? Because they want an end to killing? Who is the Christian? Was the *Peace* on our Christmas cards subversive this year?

After leaving church, the President and his wife drove around the Capital. A reporter later asked Lady Bird her opinion of the march. She said, "I was thinking, by gosh, what a big clean-up bill this city is going to face. It must be ankle deep in the trash they left. To some extent that the demonstration was the effect of affluence and permissiveness. It was about as unconstructive a work as I can remember seeing."

As I have said, I'm neither hippy nor Maoist, but I am against the war. I'm not against our government, but I feel we are wrong to be in Vietnam. I hoped that if the government were convinced that enough citizens felt this way it might be willing to lose a little military face in favor of appearing more civilized. That's why I went to Washington.

I now know that I was terribly naïve.

Now, like many others, I believe the government knows quite well that it does not belong in Vietnam, but *belong* is a word connected with right or wrong, and our presence is instead a matter of some insane expediency (and even that is, of course, open to question), just as arresting those kids was perhaps a matter of right or wrong, but pummeling some of them insensible was insane and expedient. The press picture of what happened—blaming it all on the weirdos—attempts to diffuse any significance the demonstration had: *Hell, man, they's only a bunch of nuts down theyuh. Raht? Raht!*

Something happened to many of us there Saturday and Sunday that is hard to describe, harder to explain. We went down to protest and returned ready to resist. Many, like myself, wandered over to the front steps out of curiosity, climbed the parapets because they were there. Somehow, in the course of that evening, I stopped thinking of the protesters as "those kids" (too many were adults) or even "them"—it became "us."

The weekend made believers of the sympathizers, activists of the passive. Usually, protest marches consist of a set of masturbatory fantasies stoked by rousing righteous speeches; everyone claps hands and goes home feeling *as if* something had been accomplished, the usual narcotic dysfunction that in the old days was accomplished by the communal singing of freedom songs to dissipate the need to act. This time was different. (As Oakland was different.) Many who were not anti-government now are; many who were committed to using legal channels to change governmental policy now have what they consider the governmental attitude—cynicism, violence, covertness—which they may use for the same end. There is a sense of solidarity among many, but at the same time a retreat from organization among many others. "You can't have an organization of five without one FBI snitch," one youth said to me. "I'm working alone now."

Someone said to me recently that Watts was protest, Detroit rebellion; the next step, moving out of the ghetto into *your* territory, will be revolution or war, depending on your point of view. I think something of the same is happening to the peace movement. Reason is starting to slip, and like the inmates of the concentration camps who gradually took on the values of their oppressors, I fear many are beginning to see violence as the only alternative to futile discussion. They go to protest and find their very serious and sincere efforts mocked or dismissed, by older liberals and popular press both, as the flip playings of the flower set, the phony feelings and posturings of left-wing extremists. They say, "Jesus Christ: how can we reach you? What will we have to do to make you listen?"

A lot of the kids never saw blood before, not a lot of blood, and it scared, revolted, and angered them. The first time you see someone really damaged is always traumatic; when it's one of your friends, it is more so. When you watch an official of the U.S. Department of Justice, presumably acting under orders from the Attorney General's office, club someone to the ground, club, club, and club, and then, when she stops yelling, drag her off by her hair with an expression on his face like he'd just gotten laid, you believe deep in your heart that you're right: we really can bomb villages and towns that have no military significance, not by mistake but just because they're there and we've got the bombs. *Kill the gooks; club the Commies; zap the mother—s, yum!*

No one should confuse this demonstration with the March on Washington in 1963; it is neither a continuation nor a degeneration of the civil rights movement; it is something quite different. In 1963 people were in Washington trying to be beautiful in the hope of being granted by the nice men up on the Hill what the Constitution had theoretically given decades before. This time the message read: please stop killing those people who haven't done anything to you; I'm not going to help do it; I may try to stop you doing it. 1963 protested being a victim; 1967 refused to become a killer.

Lawrence Stern said in the Washington *Post,* "The 1963 demonstration was an impassioned and respectful appeal to the man in the White House, then John F. Kennedy, to do something for the cause of racial equality in the United States. The attitude of yesterday's marchers toward Lyndon B. Johnson was almost hateful. . . . The 1967 march started as a jolly pep rally, then turned to the ugliness of the confrontation at the Pentagon. And the ugliness rather than the jollity is what will probably survive the day. . . . It is yet to be seen whether the protest achieved its purpose—to dramatize national opposition to the war in Vietnam. The melee of mudballs, rocks, and mass arrests at the end is sure to dominate newspaper and television coverage of the protest. And most Americans recoil from scenes of civil violence."

And that is the point, the subject of the protest: the very Americans who were so outraged by the few hotheads and fanatics will dismiss everything those thousands of people were trying to say, but will, rationally, do and condone far worse day after day after day ten thousand miles from home. Of course the attitude of the two groups of marchers toward Johnson and Kennedy is different: Kennedy was not *responsible* for racial intolerance, but Johnson bears the responsibility for Vietnam's escalation. Stern is right, the ugliness will be what survives the day, and not just for you, but also for the members of the Pentagon Expeditionary Force (civilian branch). As an educator, that means something to me, and I do not like it very much.

The scary part is that it is not simply a question of the Vietnam War anymore. That is why we went to the Capital, but that is not what is now important. It is something more, something worse, something far more cancerous, something of which the war is a symptom. It is this: that quaint American belief that you can say and believe what you think true is a permit that applies only before dark, only so far as it doesn't interfere with those who are in power; we realized that those in power will use any mechanism at hand to wrinkle your mind and body to shut you up, will lie and cheat and hide, they'll draft you or beat you or arrest you to shut you up, they'll lie to the press ("The demonstrators released the tear gas," said the Pentagon), and the press, which needs its news sources' goodwill, for the most part buys it because buying it avoids the hassle of having to believe and print that those citizens may be right. It is this too: that the liberals of the older generation will accept the same nonsense as a means to dismiss what happened, discharge their own anxiety over their own effeteness; that the ones you knew wouldn't leave their office but expected at least to man their typewriters are so threatened they too join the enemy.

It is also an evil I feel in the peace movement itself. "Do your own thing" is the current *cri de coeur.* I think it both reflects the malady of the movement and impedes a cure. The first thing that comes to mind on hearing the cry is that it implies great tolerance for other people's perceptions of situations and methods of coping with them, a very nice catholicism. But in this troublesome world I don't think we can afford to permit even apparently benevolent anarchy to go unexamined. Examination of this one reveals some things not particularly pleasant.

"Do your own thing" is a statement of accommodation from leaders who really cannot lead, an attempt to box uncontrol by those who cannot control. In part, it stems from the disintegration in the civil rights movement: one has a choice between true tolerance of action and open hostility to it. The danger is that there is no way to contain the cranks, the nuts, the fetishists, and no way to consolidate the gains when they do happen to occur. In rebellion, anarchy is a luxury, and I'm not sure this rebellion can afford it very well.

My fear is that putting it on the line, the literal line, be it a sit-in or a picket line, isn't good enough anymore. What is happening to the peace movement is what happened to the civil rights movement: there is that awful realization that you spend most of your time talking to yourself. SNCC used to be what its name said: Student Nonviolent Coordinating Committee. The white kids are just beginning to understand the reason for the change.

I think we all had better start understanding the change. The importance of the Pentagon encounter isn't that an easy out has been supplied with which one may now put down all the peaceniks; there is no justification for the gambit so much of the press would like—the one that would let you lump all those people together in a pink-colored Maoist hippie bag you can discard somewhere. Like the cat in the song, it comes back. It isn't the outrageous conduct of the extremists and weirdos that weekend that is important—it is nothing new for a Maoist to be hostile, for a nut to be nutty—it is what happened in the minds of those otherwise straight kids and middle-aged demonstrators. They've realized the march really was, as LBJ implied, nothing more than a terribly pathetic and futile gesture, that what was real about it were the clubs wielded by the marshals and the tear gas grenades thrown by the paratroopers. Those who went to Washington for peace now have a choice: play *that* game or quit.

There is one other course of action, one that for the present I am going to assume is still viable. Perhaps in that assumption I show my allegiance to the older generation (the kids may be right, there may be a cutoff at thirty), but even though I am almost certain legal means will not at present effect a change in our unjust and fruitless war or the way our governmental machine is beginning to react to dissent, I still want to try by working within the machinery we have. I grew up believing that Congress was rational and sincere, that the presidency was an institution more than an ego; even though I've been disabused of these childish idiocies, I am not free of them emotionally and I still have an attachment for the institutions themselves. Although I expect the attempt to be futile, I am going to try to run for Congress next year.

I am by profession a teacher and writer, and I do not like the profession of politician, but when confronted by a moral outrage such as our Vietnam involvement, talking and typing are not enough, one simply must do more; one must at least *try*. I am not able to identify with the violent resistance, nor am I lucky enough to be able to turn off consciousness of the awful evil my country is supervising and administering. Even with an enormous military that is largely covert and an administration that is largely mendacious, I think it is possible to blame the evil on evil men and believe the democratic process itself capable of permitting change for the good.

But the young people who do not entertain this romance with the American myth—what of them? I fear for them, I worry about what I see happening to them, about what I fear they will do and what we will do to them. They say to us: you brought us up to appreciate the evil the Nazis created, and in example you do the same yourselves in Vietnam; you taught us of government keyed to justice and fairness, of a free press, and in life you've shown us expediency and self-interest and a free press so committed to the same expediency it lies on its own. As great as is the current cost of the war—described so well by Reston above—I fear more the future loss: a generation of kids who will feel able to approach and deal with life in America only with the cynicism, violence, expediency, and appreciation for raw power that is now limited to the highest echelons of our government.

Postscript to "The Battle of the Pentagon"

I *did* run for Congress after this article appeared in *Atlantic.* Running for Congress wasn't anything I'd ever wanted to do, and it's not something I'll ever do again.

The antepenultimate and penultimate paragraphs of the article were written after Mike Janeway, then assistant editor at *Atlantic,* told me he thought the piece needed something more at the end: "You've told us what you think everyone else is going to do. Are you just going to write your article and leave it there? What are *you* going to do?" I told him I *had* done something about it by writing the article. "That was then. Think about it and write a paragraph or two telling us what you're going to do now."

I wrote the paragraphs saying that I was going to run for Congress, but I don't think I had any intention of actually *doing* it. I knew little about and no one in elective politics, so I knew of no way I could get into elective politics. I don't think I was lying when I wrote those paragraphs; rather, I was being hypothetical. That's what professors do: they make things hypothetical and then they don't have to *do* anything.

But other people around here did have practical knowledge of such matters, and some of them had been reading *Atlantic.* A few months after the article appeared Rayford Boddy, an economist from the university, called to say he and a few friends wanted to talk with me about something important. He was a neighbor so I told him to come on over. He and the group with him said they were ready to go to work. "At what?" I asked.

"On your campaign," Ray said. "It's time to get started."

"What campaign?"

"The one you said you were going to run in *Atlantic.*"

"Oh, *that* campaign. I don't want to do it any more," I said.

"Don't be silly," he said. "It was published in *Atlantic.* You have to do it."

The incumbent in New York's Thirty-eighth Congressional District was

Max McCarthy, a Democrat. I was also a Democrat. McCarthy was one of the first House members to make the environment a campaign issue. He was good on civil rights and poverty issues. People liked Max McCarthy. He had defeated a Republican neanderthal in a district that had been Republican for the previous two decades. How could I run against Max McCarthy?

"In the primary," Ray said. "You run against him in the primary for the nomination."

Max, Ray pointed out, was indeed a good guy but he had one fault: he had backed President Johnson on every war vote. Max had told friends, one of my visitors said, that he was personally opposed to the war but Johnson had helped him in his second campaign when the local pols had abandoned him, and he felt he owed the president a debt.

I said I would do it on one condition: this was a one-issue campaign, so if McCarthy changed his position on the war, we would swing our support to him. Everyone agreed and we set about doing it.

Herman Schwartz, with whom I was then teaching a seminar on prisoners' rights law at the University at Buffalo Law School, said he was opposed to the whole idea. "You're a professor," Herman said, "and professors aren't supposed to get *involved* in things. That's for other people. You really ought to stay out of electoral politics. People like you should be gadflies on the sidelines." I told him that even if the metaphor hadn't been mangled, I'd still disagree. "They'll chew you up," Herman said.

Many of my friends pretended it wasn't happening. It was as if I'd professed a passionate interest in professional bowling or had taken to wearing a large pearl in one ear. Their attitude seemed to be that if nothing were said the whole thing would eventually pass by without lingering embarrassment. Carl Kaysen, who had been a senior fellow during part of my four years in Harvard's Society of Fellows, and who had since become director of the Institute for Advanced Studies in Princeton, said he thought my running for Congress was an odd idea but a worthwhile enterprise. He convinced Martin Peretz to contribute to the campaign, and at that point the whole thing became real because, with Peretz's check in the bank, there was something other than words to be dealt with.

Ray Boddy arranged meetings with individuals and with groups. The first was with a group the name of which I no longer remember exactly; it was something like the People's Party for Peace and Democracy. Their leader, Frank, said they were opposed to electoral politics on principle, so they were therefore opposed to backing anyone in the Democratic primary. Things were very chilly for about fifteen minutes, then everything suddenly warmed up and Frank said they'd make an exception and work on the campaign because it sounded like fun. I asked why they were making the exception. "Because anyone who's a friend of Pete Seeger's must be all right," Frank said. I asked how he knew Seeger and I were friends. Frank smiled and winked at Ray; Ray winked back. It seemed clear that they all knew they were going to offer support all along, that the fifteen minutes of coolness was just some sort of dance they had to go through. I thanked them for their promise of support. Frank said they would put out troops to go door to door with petitions and such, the real legwork that is the heart of any political campaign. They were enormously concerned with truth, social good, and how things would appear. They could have served as template for "The People's Front of Judea," the cockamamie revolutionary party in Monty Python's *Life of Brian.*

I met with a corporate executive who had been a significant contributor to Max's previous campaign. "What should I say to him?" I asked Ray. "Just play it by ear," Ray said. "Answer his questions and you'll do okay." The apartment was dark and quiet; the curtains and carpet were thick. The man offered drinks. We sat down. I waited for his questions. "Well," he said, after what I think was a very long while, "it's your nickel." Ray looked at his shoes. I talked for about ten minutes and then we got up to go. At the door the man said, "I'm not going to give you any money because I don't know you, but I want you to know that I'm not going to give Max any money because I think he's wrong about the war. This war is just too damned evil."

"That's all I can ask," I said.

"No," he said, "you were asking for money, but this is all you're going to get." As it turned out, he went further: a week later he called to tell me he'd set up a meeting with a group of wealthy businessmen who had in the past poured a great deal of money into political campaigns in the area. We met for lunch with about the same results: they didn't offer me any money but agreed not to give Max any either.

The Liberal party said it would hear statements from the candidates from the district, and I was given a time to appear. The man who greeted me said I had ten minutes. Before I said anything someone in the back row asked a question about the university. I answered it. Someone else asked another question about the university, and I answered that question too. I started to make my statement about the election when a man in the second row leapt up and began slapping his left wrist with his right hand. He was grunting something unintelligible and I thought he was having a seizure. Then I realized that what he was grunting was "Ten! ten! ten!" The chairman said, "I'm sorry, but as Ed has pointed out, your time is up. Thank you very much for coming to speak with us. We will consider your candidacy carefully. Thank you for your statement and for explaining your positions to us." He turned away from me and it was as if I weren't even in the room.

"But I didn't get to say. . . . "

"Yes, thank you for coming to speak with us."

Later, Ray asked how the presentation had gone. "Those people are crazy," I said. He said he knew that. He told me that they would wind up endorsing an ex-cop, a strong conservative. I asked if he was sure about that. He said he was.

"Then why did you send me down there? Why waste my time?"

"Practice. It was good experience for you."

The group supporting Gene McCarthy, the Coalition for a Democratic Alternative (CDA), refused to have anything to do with my campaign. They told me that my running against Max conflicted with their campaign against President Johnson. I asked how a congressional campaign based on the same issue as Gene McCarthy's presidential campaign could do anything but help. Max, after all, was the same sort of target as Johnson: it was the war policy that made him objectionable, not the domestic issues; on domestic issues, Lyndon and Max were swell. They told me I didn't understand politics. I later learned that they didn't help me because a woman in the CDA executive committee had worked very hard for Max in the previous election. Although she would no longer work for him herself and was disgusted by his position on the war, she was still very fond of him. They didn't want to hurt her feelings by supporting me. I told them that I admired their chivalry but found their politics quixotic. They told me politics was far more complicated than I thought.

A biologist friend named Walter urged me to bring a social scientist friend of his from Minneapolis as a consultant. "It will only cost you a few hundred bucks plus his transportation." I told Walter that such a visit would consume the current contents of the war chest. "It's worth it," Walter said. "He's had experience running campaigns there. He can give you a lot of good advice." I said that perhaps if some money came in we'd consider it. "You've got to decide now," Walter said. "He's very busy and if you don't get something set up in the next few weeks, it will be impossible to do anything in time to do you any good in the primary." I didn't invite Walter's friend to Buffalo. The money wasn't there and I wasn't convinced that he had anything to say to help us. About a week later Walter's wife called to invite my wife and me to dinner. She said an old friend, now working as a political consultant in Minneapolis, was visiting them with his wife and kids. At the dinner I asked the man how come he was here this week. "Oh, we've been planning this for months. We're on our way to Boston." So Walter had just been trying to hustle me for a little extra money for his pal. I never said anything about it, but after that dinner Walter stopped coming to the campaign meetings.

I went to Washington and visited Max McCarthy. I'd never met a congressman and I was a little nervous about the encounter. Max had thick coke-bottle glasses, and he introduced me to his wife and daughter, both of whom worked in his office. I felt like an utter rat: this was about politics for me; for Max and his family, it was daily bread. He said he just couldn't turn his back on LBJ after LBJ had stood by him two years earlier. Couldn't we work something out? I couldn't think of anything. He said he doubted that there was enough Democratic money for both a primary and a fall campaign, so if we did have a primary fight the bad guys might win by default. I suggested he resign from the primary then. He said that wasn't what he had in mind.

I had a meeting at my house with twenty-five key people. A few minutes before the meeting, Frank, the head of the People's Party for Peace and Democracy arrived alone to tell me that the PPPD couldn't support me after all. "You guys were supposed to be bringing the *food* for tonight's meeting. What do you mean you can't *support* me?"

"We found out you met with ______ three days ago."

I forget who ______ was, but I remember saying, "What do you mean you found out. I *told* you a week ago I had a meeting with them."

"Right. We had a meeting to discuss it and we decided that means you sold out, so we can't support you."

"Sold out? Sold out for what? What did I get? I haven't gotten anything from any of these people. I haven't promised anything to any of these people."

"That's not what selling out means. Anyway, we're against electoral politics. You always knew that. We decided to go back to our principles."

"How can you do this to me just minutes before twenty-five people come here to discuss campaign policy and you're supposed to be bringing the food?"

"I thought you'd prefer it if I was up front. Rather than saying it in the meeting, you know? Or saying nothing at the meeting and then saying it later. We're still friends, right?"

"No, I don't think so."

"You'll see we're right when you've had time to think about it. It just wouldn't look right, us supporting a candidate in an election."

"Even if that means a pro-war candidate is elected?"

"Do the means justify the ends?" Frank clearly wanted to engage in philosophical discussion; I wanted to engage in carnage. Neither of us got what he wanted.

About a week later, Max McCarthy telephoned. He was giving a speech that night to the League of Women Voters, and he wondered if I, as an English professor, would look the typescript over and maybe correct any errors. It was crazy enough a question for me to say, "Sure, come on over."

Max came on over. My dog Lulu bit him on the ankle while I was taking his coat. "She doesn't usually do that," I said. Max sat down in the living room and handed me the draft of the speech. The gist of the speech was that Max had supported LBJ on the war for a long time because LBJ was a good man and he, Max, trusted him, but it was time for other opinions to prevail. The war was a loser in all regards, and we had to cut our losses and get out.

"You're going to give this speech?" I asked.

"Unless you think there's something in it I should change," Max said, rubbing his ankle.

"Don't change a word, Max. You give the speech and I'm out."

"Thank you," he said.

"No, thank *you.*"

After Max delivered his speech and it was clear that he had changed his position, I sent everyone involved in my campaign a letter telling them that it was over, we'd won, I was out of it, thank you all very much. I didn't tell them how happy I was to be out of it. Several wanted to talk. I didn't want to talk; I saw no point in it. One of them wondered with more than a little anger how I could refuse to agree to a talk, after all the work they'd done. We met at the CDA office. "We don't think you should drop out," one said.

"Why not?"

"Because we think you can win."

"What's to win? We agreed from the beginning that all we were after was to get a congressman who would be against the war. We've got that now."

"You don't understand: you can *beat* Max in the primary. And we think you can win in November. Once you beat Max in the primary, the money will be there, and it won't take that much to beat the other guy. You've already got Max on the run."

"No. I've already got him where we said we wanted him. I'm out."

"Will you at least think about it?"

"No."

"You owe us at least that much."

"Okay, I'll think about it." I was lying, and they knew it.

The finance committee chairman of the CDA, the Gene McCarthy group, called and said, "I hear you've got sources of money."

"For what?"

"Money you don't need now."

"I don't have any money."

"You got some contributions, I heard."

"Small ones. But we spent those organizing, and it was all over before we got a financial campaign going."

"But you still have sources."

"No, I don't."

"What about your Newport friends? You know Pete Seeger and Judy Collins and people like that. Are they giving benefits?"

"I haven't asked anyone to give benefits. I hardly know Judy Collins, and Pete is already working for Gene McCarthy."

"I hear you have other sources."

"You hear wrong. I don't have anything."

"You should give it to us. You really should."

I asked if she didn't feel a little odd calling me now, for the first time, especially after the way her group had totally ignored my campaign against Max.

"What does that matter? You don't need the money now so you should give it to us."

"Don't you listen? You didn't answer my question. Why didn't you support me when I was running as an antiwar candidate against Max?"

"That was politics. It was necessary."

"There isn't any money."

"Well, would you like to come to work for us as a fund-raiser?"

I said something vile and hung up.

I got one more call, from Frank, the leader of the People's Party for Peace and Democracy, the group that stiffed me just before the large meeting. He said that the PPPD was willing to endorse me now. I told him that Max had come around and that I had withdrawn. I told him that I'd told everyone else I was going to support Max McCarthy and that I was encouraging people to do likewise. "We know all that," he said. "That's why we want to back you. Now that you're not indebted to anyone you can run as an independent. You don't stand a chance of winning anyway. It will be fantastic."

"What's the point of running as an independent when you know you can't win and there's no political reason for running in the first place?"

"I told you, we're opposed to electoral politics. Winning isn't the issue. We can make an incredible statement. It's a great opportunity: to have a campaign free of the burden of—"

"I don't think I've got what it takes for electoral politics," I said.

"You can learn," he said. "I'll teach you."

"I don't think so," I said. . . .

The antiwar demonstrations of 1967 contributed to Eugene McCarthy's strong showing in the 1968 New Hampshire primary, which in turn led to Lyndon B. Johnson's withdrawal from the race and Robert Kennedy's decision to run. But the peace candidates didn't win that election; they didn't come close. Gene McCarthy never had a real chance for the Democratic nomination, and Bobby Kennedy was murdered, so the nomination went to Hubert Humphrey, who wouldn't disassociate himself from Johnson on the war issue or from Chicago Mayor Richard Daley after the savage police attack on unarmed and nonviolent antiwar demonstrators. The Chicago violence was on prime-time national television, and it probably cost Humphrey the presidency. Many Democrats, not just war opponents, sulked the election out in protest, and Richard Nixon won by a slim margin. The majority of American and Vietnamese war deaths occurred during Nixon's presidency.

I wonder if things would have been any different had our protests not been so comfortable, so often a matter of convenience. In the antiwar movement, we knew a long time in advance when an event was coming along in which we might take part. That allowed us to tune our schedules so participation caused relatively little disruption in ordinary life. There was none of the long-term hardship we saw in Tiananmen Square: hardly anyone went to an antiwar demonstration and put ordinary life on hold for the duration. There were frequent teargassings and there was the police riot in Chicago, but major violence was rare. The real American domestic brutality in those years was by local police and Klan groups against civil rights workers; federal brutality was concentrated in Southeast Asia. No one died at the Pentagon demonstration in October 1967 or, except for Kent State, at any of the other major antiwar demonstrations. The government preferred to use the courts and agents provocateurs funded and controlled by the FBI's COINTELPRO operation to harass individuals and groups who seemed to be accomplishing something. Most people were not harassed or even inconvenienced very much. Ordinarily, we went to our marches by car, train, plane, or chartered bus, and we went home that night or the next day. We hardly ever missed school or work. It was an adventure, an adrenalin high with a soupçon of risk. It was a good thing to do, it probably made some differences in American life, but finally it was probably exhaustion, not good sense or decency, that got us out of that war.

I can't help but wonder what would have happened if, like the students at Tiananmen Square and like so many of the civil rights workers in the American South, we had gone and just stayed there. Would the government have ignored us the way it ignored the campers of the Poor People's Campaign in 1969? Would the president have ordered troops to run us out with bayonets and gunfire, the way the Chinese government did in Tiananmen Square and the way Herbert Hoover did with the veterans' Bonus Army on the Anacostia Flats? In November 1969 there was another big antiwar march in Washington. President Nixon had the White House completely encircled by a barrier of bumper-to-bumper yellow school buses. He was shown on television watching a football game. What if we hadn't all gone home that Sunday night, if we had stayed through the week when Nixon's football game was over and the school buses had other jobs to do?

The past is a fact, absolutely ineluctable; there are no "what ifs" in real life. But you can always think about next time. For a long time I liked to think that next time we would stay longer, but now that may be a pointless hope: the last two American administrations drew lessons from Vietnam that may very well preclude such peaceful opposition. Our three most recent military campaigns—against Grenada, Panama, and Iraq—deployed and utilized massive military firepower against vastly inferior forces, and each campaign was over in a matter of days. In each of those military campaigns the press was strictly controlled and censored by the U.S. government. It was an astonishingly efficient way to foreclose an informed opposition: stage a rapid war against a much weaker opponent with only a small amount of censored information allowed out while the war is going on. Disturbing facts may come out later, but people don't organize demonstrations over disturbing facts when nobody is being blown up. They just write articles and talk about it.

White-Collar Pill Party

(*Atlantic Monthly,* 1966)

This article is primarily about illegal amphetamine use by middle-class professionals in the mid-1960s. If we changed all the references to "pills" to "cocaine," it could, with only a few other changes, be about cocaine use in the same socioeconomic group in the past decade.

Before the recent cocaine frenzy, most law enforcement, social agency, and press attention to the "drug problem" focused on lower-class street users. I've long thought that focus incorrect. The two primary drugs of abuse in America, the drugs that have the most addicts and cause the most harm, are and have been alcohol and tobacco. Alcohol is a significant agent in most violent crimes and automobile and industrial accidents; cigarettes kill more people every year than violent criminals. Their abuse is by no means limited to the urban poor or to people whose names end in vowels.

The "four-year-old son, Michael" mentioned in the opening paragraphs of this article is now a practicing attorney. When he was in his late teens he interviewed middle-class kids in our part of New York State about their drug use. The interviews were published as *Doing Drugs* (Jackson and Jackson, 1983).

There was a thing called Heaven; but all the same they used to drink enormous quantities of alcohol. . . . There was a thing called the soul and a thing called immortality. . . . But they used to take morphia and cocaine. . . . Two thousand pharmacologists and bio-chemists were subsidized in A.F. 178. . . . Six years later it was being produced commercially. The perfect drug. . . . Euphoric, narcotic, pleasantly hallucinant. . . . All the advantages of Christianity and alcohol; none of their defects. . . . Take a holiday from reality whenever you like, and come back without so much as a headache or a mythology.

Aldous Huxley, *Brave New World,* 1932

DRUGS, LIKE CHEWING GUM, TV, oversize cars, and crime, are part of the American way of life. No one receives an exemption.

This was made particularly clear to me recently by my four-year-old son, Michael, who came into the kitchen one evening and asked me to go out and buy a certain brand of vitamin pills for him. Since he is quite healthy and not observably hypochondriac, I asked why he wanted them. "So I can be as strong as Jimmy down the block."

"There isn't any Jimmy down the block," I said, whereupon he patiently explained that the clown on the 5 P.M. TV program he watches every day had *told* him the pills would make him stronger than Jimmy, and his tone gave me to understand that the existence of a corporeal Jimmy was irrelevant: the truehearted clown, the child's friend, had advised the pills, and any four-year-old knows a clown wouldn't steer you wrong.

For adults the process is modified slightly. An afternoon TV commercial urges women to purchase a new drug for their "everyday headache" (without warning them that anyone who has a headache every day should certainly be consulting a GP or a psychiatrist); a Former Personality with suggestive regularity tells you to keep your bloodstream pure by consuming buffered aspirin for the headache you are supposed to have, and another recommends regular doses of iron for your "tired blood." (It won't be long before another screen has-been mounts the TV commercial podium with a pill that doesn't do anything at all; it just keeps your corpuscles company on the days you ate liver and forgot to have a headache.)

One result of all the drug propaganda and the appalling faith in the efficacy of drugs is that a lot of people take a lot more pills than they have any reason to. They think in terms of pills. And so do their physicians: you fix a fat man by giving him a diet pill, you fix a chronic insomniac by giving him a sleeping pill. But these conditions are frequently merely symptoms of far more complicated disorders. The convenient prescription blank solves the problem of finding out what the trouble really is—it makes the symptom seem to go away.

Think for a moment: how many people do you know who cannot stop stuffing themselves without an amphetamine and who cannot go to sleep without a barbiturate (over *nine billion* of those produced last year) or make it through a workday without a sequence of tranquilizers? And what about those six million alcoholics, who daily ingest quantities of what is, by sheer force of numbers, the most addicting drug in America?

The publicity goes to the junkies, lately to the college kids, but these account for only a small portion of the American drug problem. Far more worrisome are the millions of people who have become dependent on commercial drugs. The junkie *knows* he is hooked; the housewife on amphetamine and the businessman on meprobamate hardly ever realize what has gone wrong.

Sometimes the pill takers meet other pill takers, and an odd thing happens: instead of using the drug to cope with the world, they begin to use their time to take drugs. Taking drugs becomes *something to do.* When this stage is reached, the drug-taking pattern broadens: the user takes a wider variety of drugs with increasing frequency. For want of a better term, one might call it the white-collar drug scene.

I first learned about it during a party in Chicago last winter, and the best way to introduce you will be to tell you something about that evening, the people I met, what I think was happening.

There were about a dozen people in the room, and over the noise from the record player scraps of conversation came through:

"Now the Desbutal, if you take it with this stuff, has a peculiar effect, contraindication, at least it did for me. You let me know if you . . . "

"I don't have one legitimate prescription, Harry, not *one!* Can you imagine that?" "I'll get you some tomorrow, dear."

" . . . and this pharmacist on Fifth will sell you all the leapers [amphetamines] you can carry—just like that. Right off the street. I don't think he'd know a prescription if it bit him." "As long as he can read the labels, what the hell."

"You know, a funny thing happened to me. I got this green and yellow capsule, and I looked it up in the Book, and it wasn't anything I'd been using, and I thought, great! It's not something I've built a tolerance to. And I took it. A couple of them. And you know what happened? *Nothing!* That's what happened, not a goddamned thing."

The Book—the *Physicians' Desk Reference,* which lists the composition and effects of almost all commercial pharmaceuticals produced in this country—passes back and forth, and two or three people at a time look up the contents and possible values of a drug one of them has just discovered or heard about or acquired or taken. The Book is the pillhead's *Yellow Pages:* you look up the effect you want ("Sympathomimetics" or "Cerebral Stimulants," for example), and it tells you the magic columns. The pillheads swap stories of kicks and sound like professional chemists discussing recent developments; others listen, then examine the *PDR* to see if the drug discussed really could do that.

Eddie, the host, a painter who has received some recognition, had been awake three or four days, he was not exactly sure. He consumes between 150 and 200 milligrams of amphetamine a day, needs a large part of that to stay awake, even when he has slipped a night's sleep in somewhere. The dose would cause most people some difficulty; the familiar diet pill, a capsule of Dexamyl or Eskatrol, which makes the new user edgy and overenergetic and slightly insomniac the first few days, contains only 10 or 15 milligrams of amphetamine. But amphetamine is one of the few central nervous system stimulants to which one can develop a tolerance, and over the months and years Ed and his friends have built up massive tolerances and dependencies. "Leapers aren't so hard to give up," he told me. "I mean, I sleep almost constantly when I'm off, but you get over that. But everything is so damned boring without the pills."

I asked him if he knew many amphetamine users who have given up the pills.

"For good?"

I nodded.

"I haven't known anybody that's given it up for good." He reached out and took a few pills from the candy dish in the middle of the coffee table, then washed them down with some Coke.

The last couple to arrive—a journalist and his wife—settled into positions. The wife was next to me on the oversize sofa, and she skimmed through the "Product Identification Section" of the *PDR,* dozens of pages of pretty color photos of tablets and capsules. "Hey!" she said to no one in particular. Then, to her husband, "Look at the pretty hexagonal. George, get the Source to get some of them for me." George, across the table, near the fire, nodded.

I had been advised to watch him as he turned on. As the pills took effect something happened to the muscles of his face, and the whole assembly seemed to go rubbery. His features settled lower and more loosely on the bones of his head. He began to talk with considerably more verve.

A distractingly pretty girl with dark brown eyes sat at the edge of our group and ignored both the joint making its rounds and the record player belching away just behind her. Between the thumb and middle finger of her left hand she held a pill that was blue on one side and yellow on the other; steadily, with the double-edged razor blade she held in her right hand, she sawed on the seam between the two halves of the pill. Every once in a while she rotated it a few degrees with her left index finger. Her skin was smooth, and the light from the fireplace played tricks with it, all of them charming. The right hand sawed on.

I got the Book from the coffee table and looked for the pill in the pages of color pictures, but before I found it, Ed leaned over and said, "They're Desbutal Gradumets. Abbott Labs."

I turned to the "Professional Products Information" section and learned that Desbutal is a combination of Desoxyn (methamphetamine hydrochloride, also marketed as Methedrine) and Nembutal, that the pill the girl sawed contained 15 milligrams of the Dexosyn, that the combination of drugs served "to both stimulate and calm the patient so that feelings of depression are overcome and a sense of well-being and increased energy is produced. Inner tension and anxiety are relieved so that a sense of serenity and ease of mind prevails." Gradumets, the Book explained, "are indicated in the management of obesity, the management of depressed states, certain behavioral syndromes, and a number of typical geriatric conditions," as well as "helpful in managing psychosomatic complaints and neuroses," Parkinson's disease, and a hangover.

The girl, obviously, was not interested in all of the pill's splendid therapeutic promises; were she, she would not have been so diligently sawing along that seam. She was after the methamphetamine, which like other amphetamines "depresses appetite, elevates the mood, increases the urge to work, imparts a sense of increased efficiency, and counteracts sleepiness and the feeling of fatigue in most persons."

After what seemed a long while the pill split into two round sections. A few scraps of the yellow Nembutal adhered to the Desoxyn side, and she carefully scraped them away. "Wilkinson's the best blade for this sort of thing," she said. I asked if she didn't cut herself on occasion, and she showed me a few nicks in her left thumb. "But a single edge isn't thin enough to do it neatly."

She put the blue disk in one small container, the yellow in another, then from a third took a fresh Desbutal and began sawing. I asked why she kept the Nembutal, since it was the Desoxyn she was after.

"Sometimes I might want to sleep, you know. I might *have* to sleep because something is coming up the next day. It's not easy for us to sleep, and sometimes we just don't for a couple or three days. But if we have to, we can just take a few of these." She smiled at me tolerantly, then returned to her blade and tablet.

When I saw Ed in New York several weeks later, I asked about her. "Some are like that," he said; "they like to carve on their pills. She'll sit and carve for thirty or forty minutes."

"Is that sort of ritual an important part of it all?"

"I think it is. She seems to have gotten hung up on it. I told her that she shouldn't take that Nembutal, that I have been cutting the Nembutal off my pills. It only takes about thirty seconds. And she can spend a good half hour at it if she has a mind to. I told her once about the effect of taking a Spansule; you know, one of those big things with sustained release [like Dexamyl, a mixture of dextroamphetamine sulfate and amobarbital designed to be effective over a twelve-hour period]. What you do is open the capsule and put it in a little bowl and grind up the little pellets until it's powder, then stuff all the powder back in the pill and take it, and it all goes off at once. I'll be damned if I haven't seen her grinding away like she was making matzo meal. That's a sign of a fairly confirmed head when they reach that ritual stage."

Next to the candy dish filled with Dexedrine, Dexamyl, Eskatrol, Desbutal, and a few other products I hadn't yet learned to identify, near the five-pound box of Dexedrine tablets someone had brought, were two bottles. One was filled with Dexedrine Elixir, the other with Dexamyl Elixir. Someone took a long swallow from the latter, and I thought him to be an extremely heavy user, but when the man left the room, a lawyer told me he'd bet the man was new at it. "He has to be. A mouthful is like two pills, and if he was a real head, he'd have a far greater tolerance to the Dexedrine than the amobarbital, and the stuff would make him sleepy. Anyhow, I don't like to mess with barbiturates much anymore. Dorothy Kilgallen died from that." He took a drink from the Dexedrine bottle and said, "And this tastes better. Very tasty stuff, like cherry syrup. Make a nice cherry Coke with it. The Dexamyl Elixir is bitter."

Someone emptied the tobacco from a Salem and filled the tube with grass; he tamped it down with a Tinkertoy stick, crimped the tip, then lighted it and inhaled noisily. He immediately passed the joint to the person on his left. Since one must hold the smoke in one's lungs for several seconds to get the full effect, it is more economical for several people to turn on at once. The grass was very good and seemed to produce a quiet but substantial high. One doesn't notice it coming on, but there is a realization that for a while now the room has been a decidedly pleasant one, and some noises are particularly interesting for their own sake.

I leaned back and closed my eyes for a moment. It was almost 5 A.M., and in three hours I had to catch a plane at O'Hare. "You're not going to *sleep* are you?" The tone implied that this group considered few human frailties truly gauche, but going to sleep was surely one of them. I shook my head no and looked to see who had spoken. It was Ed's wife; she looked concerned. "Do you want a pill?" I shook my head no again.

Then, just then, I realized that Ed—who knew I was not a pill-user—had not once in the evening offered me one of the many samples that had been passed around, nor had anyone else. Just the grass, but not the pills. His wife suggested a pill not so that I might get high, but merely so that I could stay awake without difficulty.

"I'm not tired," I said, "just relaxing." I assured her I wouldn't doze off. She was still concerned, however, and got me a cup of coffee from the kitchen and offered some Murine from her purse.

The front door opened, and there was a vicious blast of winter off Lake Michigan. Ed kicked the door closed behind him and dumped an armful of logs by the fireplace, then went back into the kitchen. A moment later he returned and passed around a small dish of capsules. And this time it was handed to me. They looked familiar. "One-a-Days," he said. I had learned enough from the Book to see the need for them: the amphetamine user often does not eat for long periods of time (some days his only nourishment is the sugar in the bottles of soda which he drinks to wash down the pills and counter their side effect of dehydration of the mouth), and he not only tends to lose weight but also risks vitamin deficiencies. After a while, the heavy user learns to force-feed himself or go off pills every once in a while in order to eat without difficulty and to keep his tolerance level down.

Later, getting settled in the plane, I thought, What a wild party that was. I'd never been to anything quite like it, and I began making notes about what had gone on. Not long before we came into Logan, it suddenly struck me that there had been nothing wild about the party at all, nothing. There had been women there, some of them unaccompanied and some with husbands or dates, but there had been none of the playing around and sexual hustling that several years of academic and business world parties had led me to consider a correlative of almost any evening gathering of more than ten men and women: no meaningful looks, no wisecracks, no "accidental" rubbing. No one had spoken loudly, no one had become giggly or silly, no one had lost control or seemed anywhere near it. Viewed with some perspective, the evening seemed nothing more than comfortable.

There are various ways to acquire the pills, but the most common is also the most legal: prescriptions. Even though there is now a federal law requiring physicians and pharmacists to maintain careful records regarding prescriptions for drugs like Dexamyl, many physicians are careless about prescribing them, and few seem to realize that the kind of personality that needs them is often the kind of personality that can easily acquire an overwhelming dependency on them. Often a patient will be issued a refillable prescription; if the patient is a heavy user, all he needs to do is visit several physicians and get refillable prescriptions from each. If he is worried that a cross-check of druggists' lists might turn up his name, he can easily give some of his doctors false names.

There are dealers, generically called the Source, who specialize in selling these drugs; some give them away. They do not seem to be underworld types but professional people in various capacities who, for one reason or another, have access to large quantities of them. If one is completely without connections, the drugs can be made at home. One young man I know made mescaline, amphetamine, methamphetamine, LSD, and DET and DMT (diethyl- and dimethyltryptamine, hallucinogens of shorter duration and greater punch than LSD) in his kitchen. In small lots, dextroamphetamine sulfate costs him about 50 cents a gram; a pound costs him about $30 (the same amounts of Dexedrine at your friendly corner druggist's would cost, respectively, about $10 and $4,200).

In some areas, primarily those fairly distant from major centers of drug distribution, the new law has begun to have some significant effect. In one medium-sized city, for example, the price of black-market Dexamyl and Eskatrol Spansules has risen from 15 cents to 50 cents a capsule, when one can connect for them at all.

In the major cities one can still connect, but it is becoming more difficult. The new law will inhibit, but there may be complications. It would be unfortunate if the price should be driven up so high that it would become profitable for criminal organizations to involve themselves with the traffic, as was the case with opiates in the 1940s and 1950s and alcohol in the 1920s.

There was talk in Manhattan last winter, just before the new law took effect, that some LSD factories were closing down, and I know that some Sources stopped supplying. For a short time the price of LSD went up; then things stabilized, competition increased, a new packaging method developed popularity (instead of the familiar sugar cubes, one now takes one's dose on a tiny slip of paper; like a spitball, only you don't spit it out), and now the price for a dose of LSD is about 20 percent *less* than it was a year ago.

Since most of the pillheads I'm talking about are middle-class and either professional or semiprofessional, they will still be able to obtain their drugs. Their drugs of choice have a legitimate use, and it is unlikely that the government's attempt to prevent diversion will be more than partially successful. If our narcotics agents have been unable to keep off the open market drugs which have no legitimate use at all—heroin and marijuana—it hardly seems likely that they will be able to control chemicals legitimately in the possession of millions of citizens. I asked one amphetamine head in the Southwest how local supplies had been affected by the new law. "I heard about that law," he said, "but I haven't seen anybody getting panicked." Another user tells me prices have risen slightly, but not enough yet to present difficulties.

There are marked differences between these drug users and the ones who make the newspapers. They're well educated (largely college graduates), are older (25 to 40), and middle-class (with a range of occupations: writers, artists, lawyers, TV executives, journalists, political aides, housewives). They're not like the high school kids who are after a kick in any form (some of them rather illusory, as one psychosomatic gem reported to me by a New Jersey teenager: "What some of the kids do is take a cigarette and saturate it with perfume or hairspray. When this is completely soaked in and dry, they cup the cigarettes and inhale every drag. Somehow this gives them a good high"), or college students experimenting with drugs as part of a romantic program of self-location. The kids take drugs "because it's cool" and to get high, but when you talk to them you find that most ascribe the same general high to a wide range of drugs having quite diverse effects; they're promiscuous and insensitive. There is considerable evidence to suggest that almost none of the college drug users take anything illegal after graduation, for most of them lose their connections and their curiosity.

It is not likely that many of the thousands of solitary amphetamine abusers would join these groups. They take drugs to *avoid* deviance—so they can be fashionably slim, or bright and alert and functional, or so they can muster the *quoi que* with which to face the tedium of housework or some other dull job—and the last thing they want is membership in a group defined solely by one clear form of rule-breaking behavior. Several of the group members were first turned on by physicians, but a larger number were turned on by friends. Most were after a particular therapeutic effect, but after a while interest developed in the drug for its own sake and the effect became a cause, and after that the pattern of drug-taking overcame the pattern of taking a specific drug.

Some of the socialized amphetamine users specialize. One takes Dexedrine and Dexamyl almost exclusively; he takes other combinations only when he is trying to reduce his tolerance to Dexamyl. Though he is partly addicted to the barbiturates, they do not seem to trouble him very much, and on the few occasions when he has had to go off drugs (as when he was in California for a few months and found getting legal prescriptions too difficult and for some reason didn't connect with a local Source), he has had no physiological trouble giving them up. He did, of course, suffer from the overwhelming depression and enervation that characterize amphetamine withdrawal. Most heads will use other drugs along with amphetamine—especially marijuana—in order to appreciate the heightened alertness they've acquired; some alternate with hallucinogens.

To the heroin addict, the square is anyone who does not use heroin. For the dedicated pillhead there is a slightly narrower definition: the square is someone who has an alcohol dependency; those who use nothing at all aren't even classified. The boozers do bad things, they get drunk and lose control and hurt themselves and other people. They contaminate their tubes, and whenever they get really far out, they don't even remember it the next day. The pillhead's disdain is sometimes rather excessive. One girl, for example, was living with a fellow who, like her, was taking over 500 milligrams of amphetamine a day. They were getting on well. One night the two were at a party, and instead of chewing pills, her man had a few beers; the girl was furious, betrayed, outraged. Another time, at a large party that sprawled through a sprawling apartment, a girl had been on scotch and grass and she went to sleep. There were three men in the room, none of them interested in her sexually, yet they jeered and wisecracked as she nodded off. It was 4 or 5 A.M. of a Sunday, not too unreasonable a time to be drowsy. When they saw she was really asleep—breaking the double taboo by having drunk too much scotch and been put to sleep by it—they muttered a goddamn and went into another room; she was too depressing to have around.

There is an important difference in the drug-use patterns of the pillhead and opiate dependent: the latter is interested only in getting his drug and avoiding withdrawal; the former is also interested in perceiving his drugs' effects. I remember one occasion attended by someone who had obtained a fairly large mixed bag. In such a situation a junkie would have shot himself insensible; this fellow gave most of his away to his friends. With each gift he said something about a particular aspect of the drug which he found interesting. The heroin user is far less social. His stuff is too hard to get, too expensive, his withdrawal too agonizing. But the pillhead is an experimenter. Often he seems to be interested as much in observing himself experiencing reactions as he is in having the reactions.

A large part of the attractiveness may be the ritual associated with this kind of group drug abuse: the *PDR* (a holy book), the Source (the medicine man whose preparations promise a polychromatic world of sensory and mystical experiences), the sharing of proscribed materials in a closed community, the sawing and grinding, the being privy to the Pythian secrets of colors and milligrams and trade names and contra-indications and optimum dosages. And, of course, using drugs is something of a fad.

But there are costs. Kicks are rarely free in this world, and drugs are no exception. One risks dysfunction; one can go out of one's head; one may get into trouble with the police. Though the users are from a socioeconomic class that can most likely beat a first offense at almost anything, there is the problem that legal involvement of any kind, whether successfully prosecuted or not, can cause considerable embarrassment; an arrest for taking drugs may be negligible to a slum dweller in New York, but it is quite something else for a lawyer or reporter. And there is always the most tempting danger of all: getting habituated to drugs to such a degree that the drugs are no longer something extra in life but are instead a major goal.

One user wrote me, "Lately I find myself wishing not that I might kick the lunatic habit—but simply that our drug firms would soon develop something NEW which might refresh the memory of the flash and glow of that first voom-voom pill." I had asked him why take them at all, and he wrote, "I don't know. Really. Why smoke, drink, drive recklessly, sunbathe, fornicate, shoot tigers, climb mountains, gamble, lie, steal, cheat, kill, make war—and blame it all largely on our parents. Possibly to make oneself more acceptable to oneself."

Many of the pillheads are taking drugs not *only* to escape but also to have an experience that is entirely one's own. There is no one else to be propitiated, there are no explanations or excuses needed for what happens inside one's own head when one is turned on; words won't do, and that is as much a benefit as a disadvantage, because if you cannot describe, then neither can you discuss or question or submit to evaluation. The benefit and the risk are entirely one's own. Indiana University sociologist John Gagnon pointed out at a drug symposium held at Antioch College last year, "I'd like to argue that possibly in our attempt to protect people, we have underrepresented the real payoff for drug-taking as an experience, as a risk people want to run."

You select your own risks—that's what living is all about. For some of these drug users, the risks currently being marketed do not have very much sales appeal: going South for the summer with SNCC is out because they feel that they are too old and that ofays aren't much wanted anyhow; going to Vietnam for Lyndon is absurd. So they go inside. A scarier place, but no one else can muddle around with it.

There is nothing *wrong* with using chemicals to help cope with life. That is one of the things science is supposed to do, help us cope, and the business of living can be rough at times. And we have the requisite faith: I am sure that far more Americans believe in the efficacy of a pill than believe in God. The problem arises when one's concern shifts so that life becomes an exercise in coping with the chemicals.

I think there has been an unfortunate imbalance in the negative publicity. For years the press has printed marvelous tales about all the robberies and rapes performed by evil beings whose brain tissue had been jellied by heroin. But it has rarely printed stories that point out that opiates make even the randiest impotent, or that alcohol, which has five hundred times as many addicts, is an important factor in sex offenses and murders.

Lately, attention has been focused on drug abuse and experimentation among college students. Yet all the college students and all the junkies account for only a small portion of American drug abuse. The adults, the respectable grown-ups, the nice people who cannot or will not make it without depending on a variety of drugs, present a far more serious problem. For them the drug experience threatens to disrupt or even destroy life patterns and human relationships that required many years to establish.

And the problem is not a minor one. Worse, it seems to be accelerating. As Ed advised one night, "You better research the hell out of it because I'm convinced that the next ruling generation is going to be all pillheads. I'm convinced of it. If they haven't dysfunctioned completely to the point where they can't stand for office. It's getting to be unbelievable. I've never seen such a transformation in just four or five years. . . . "

Hard Time

(*Texas Monthly,* 1978)

In 1978 the Texas Department of Corrections (TDC) operated 14 prisons holding some 23,000 inmates, 92 of whom were on Death Row awaiting execution; as I am writing on this spring day in 1991, TDC consists of 35 regular and 4 private prisons, with a count of 46,828 men and women, 341 under death sentences. When I first visited TDC in 1964 the count was slightly less than 12,000; the system now has nearly 13,000 custodial officers alone. With its inmate count doubling every thirteen or fourteen years, Texas prisons are a major growth industry, and they aren't alone in that regard: on the last day of 1989 the nation's state prisons held 610,000 prisoners, compared to 190,717 inmates in 1973 (Langan, 1991:1568–69).

Most states and the federal prison system pay inmates for labor in the fields or in factories or at maintenance jobs; Texas officials have always said that they pay with time off. Texas prisoners get time off their sentences for work, school attendance, and trusty status. In 1978 prisoners could earn two days good time for every day actually served; they now can earn three days good time for every day served, which means a thirty-year sentence can be served in ten years, even without parole. Several reasons are given for the doubling of good time, but the most important is the most obvious: it's one way to relieve some of the overcrowding.

The federal district court decision in *Ruiz et al. v. Estelle,* the prisoners' rights case that came to trial in 1978, resulted in massive changes in the way TDC operates. Among other things, Judge William Wayne Justice found that Texas prison administrators were depending on brutal convict "building tenders" to maintain control of the prisons and that prison overcrowding was intolerable. In the most sweeping prison reform court order in U.S. history, Justice imposed strict controls on the way the TDC operated and on how the actions of its officials would be monitored. He ordered TDC to hire far more guards and to stop packing three inmates in one-person cells. Texans paid for these overdue reforms: the 1978–79 prison budget was less than $120 million; the 1990–91 budget was $1.45 billion. The building tenders were taken out quickly, but it was several years before TDC had trained enough guard staff to deal with the ever-expanding prisoner population. In the interim the level of inmate violence escalated rapidly, and for the first time Texas prisons had convict gangs exerting significant control over groups of weaker unaffiliated inmates. Murders of convicts by other convicts and convict assaults of guards both increased more than tenfold (Reavis, 1985). After two changes in the top administration, the internal violence began to decline. Ellis remains the most stringent among the several maximum security units in the Texas Department of Corrections.

AT FIVE IN THE AFTERNOON, two long trains of wagons drive in from the fields, returning the convicts who have been working there all day to the Ellis Unit of the Texas Department of Corrections. On either side of the wagons, armed guards wearing spurs and cowboy hats ride on horseback, making sure the trip back from the fields goes exactly as it should. At the prison gate, the guards dismount. The horses trot back to their stables. A man in the guard tower lowers a small box on a rope, the guards unload their pistols and put them in the box, and the man in the tower hauls the box up.

Squad by squad, twenty-five or thirty men at a time, the convicts are counted in and returned to the custody of the building staff. They move quickly through the gate and into the prison yard, where they take off their clothes and dump them into large laundry carts. Naked, they stand in orderly rows waiting to be searched for weapons and contraband. At the head of each row stands a guard. As each man comes to the head of his row he throws out his arms like a crucifix for a moment while the guard looks him over, then moves on when the guard nods his approval.

Another day's work is over on the Ellis Line.

Ellis is an immaculately manicured and precisely worked farm in Walker County, about eleven miles north of Huntsville. The Line does the field work there. All penitentiaries are warehouses of losers; Ellis is where Texas sends the biggest losers it has. And the biggest losers at Ellis work on the Line.

All penitentiaries are defined by the limits they place on freedom; Ellis allows less freedom than any prison I have ever known. The guards are not brutal, the convicts are not permitted to do violence to one another, the work is not exhausting. But there is never any doubt that Ellis is an institution where the authorities have complete control. Even when there is a rare inmate strike—as happened in October after the start of the *Ruiz et al. v. Estelle* prison conditions trial in Houston—it takes place in terms acceptable to the administration. The standards of behavior at Ellis are unambiguous and they are rarely violated; violation incurs predictable sanctions. Ellis is a place with few surprises.

The toughest prisons in New York, Illinois, and California have convict gangs with which the wardens must negotiate any major policy changes. There are no convict gangs at Ellis or any other Texas prison, and whenever the administrators want to make changes, the changes occur quickly and efficiently. There are many prisons in Northern states where wardens and guards never enter the cellblocks because they are afraid of what might happen to them. Such terror is unthinkable at Ellis. "The day I'm afraid to go anywhere in here anytime," says R. M. Cousins, the Ellis warden, "that's the day I quit."

On the whole, the inmates at Ellis have been in Texas Department of Corrections (TDC) facilities more times and are doing longer sentences than the inmates at any of the system's twelve other prisons for adult males. Ellis has a large portion of the men doing over fifty years, a third of the lifers, and all of the men sentenced to death. It is the prison where the Department of Corrections keeps the convicts it considers most dangerous, and the prison where inmates most in need of protection are sent for safekeeping. Some Ellis inmates argue that they aren't bad enough for Ellis. The choice is not theirs to make.

Ellis is the most orderly of public institutions. Nothing is out of place. Clutter is transitory, removed in moments. There are no cigarette butts on the floors, no unmopped spills, no dusty surfaces, no oil stains, no graffiti. There is no unemptied ashtray, no windowpane smudged with fingerprints. Every spittoon is polished. When the industrial shops begin production each weekday morning, they are perfectly clean and every tool is exactly where it is supposed to be.

Outside, the fence posts run for miles in perfect perpendiculars and parallels. The flower beds along the prison road that leads in from the county highway are weedless and immaculate. The long, splendid lines of bracketing redbuds are of uniform size and shape.

The main compound is within a double rectangle of parallel Cyclone fences. At each corner of the perimeter and at two midpoints are tall guard towers called pickets. Armed guards still man the center pickets, but the others are empty. Human eyes have been replaced by an underground detection system that sets off alarms whenever anything heavier than a small dog moves across the grass. Ten years ago a small herd of tame deer lived inside the fences and a family of mouflon sheep wandered around the inner yard. They are gone now, victims of technology—they drove the detection system crazy.

The central corridor of the main building is a quarter mile long. In the middle are two thick perpendicular wings. One houses the administrative offices and leads out to the free world; the other holds the two enormous mess halls, the kitchens, and the power plant. To reach the main hallway from the administrative wing, it is necessary to pass through a small area bracketed by two iron gates, both of which are never opened at the same time.

The other twelve wings perpendicular to the corridor—six facing pairs on each side of the long middle—are the cellblocks and dormitories. At one end of the corridor is the gymnasium, which also serves as auditorium and movie theater; at the far end, four football fields away, is the chapel.

Death Row is in one of the wings nearest the gymnasium. A guard sits just inside the barred door, logging everyone and everything in and out. He logs visitors, food trays, doctors, chaplains; he notes when the 92 condemned men take showers, who gets shaved when, whether they accept meals, and when the mail arrives. Two rows of television sets bolted to the wall outside the cells show programs and commercials from another world. To the right, through a special door, is a small caged exercise yard, built especially for and used only by the condemned men. The Death House is back in Huntsville, but it has only eight cells, a remnant of the days when the condemned arrived rarely and were sent along quickly. Now there is not enough room for the condemned, even in the special cellblock at Ellis, and the men sentenced to death there are stacked up like planes over O'Hare on a Friday evening, waiting for reversal or reprieve or death.

Many men pass close to Death Row when they're going to or coming from the gym, but there is no pausing to say hello to anyone inside. Death Row inmates are locked in one-man cells, so there is no one to see but the guard at the logging desk, and he is not chatty.

Even in the rest of the prison, there is no hanging out in the hall or anywhere else. You don't see small groups of convicts off to the side, wheeling and dealing for hours. Ellis is quiet. Men rarely shout or cheer or scream. The massive barred steel doors that section off the central corridor and the entrances to the twelve cellblocks and dormitories are eased, not slammed, shut. The aluminum messhall trays are gently stacked, the machines and hinges are well oiled, the dayroom television sets do not blare. In the evenings and on weekends, the loudest noise is often the clacking of plastic dominoes on the iron game tables.

The cells at Ellis are undecorated. No pictures of families or saints are tacked to the walls and no centerfolds from *Playboy* or *Penthouse* are taped to the undersides of the upper bunks. Personal objects are seen only from the inside looking out: a narrow shelf over each cell door holds the prisoner's personal books, stationery, tobacco, court papers, and packets of correspondence.

For all this order, there is little overt supervision. In all the large industrial shops, there are hundreds of inmates with sharp tools and heavy instruments, but hardly ever is more than one custodial officer in sight. Such a situation would be inconceivable in a San Quentin or Attica or Joliet.

Ellis has almost 2,400 inmates, and slightly less than half of them are assigned to the Line.

The Line is the heart of the Ellis system. Texas prisons are heavily industrialized now—they make license plates for Texas and several other states, cloth, leather goods, furniture, garments, mattresses; they rebuild publicly owned vehicles that are nearly junk; they computerize many of the state's records. But the Line feeds everyone, and it is because of the Line that Texas can maintain its convicts at a budgeted cost of $7.25 per day per man, a fourth or fifth of what prison systems in the North pay to keep a man locked up.

The Line grows all the food. The Line supplies the raw materials for the garment factories. The Line grows the grain to feed the cattle that are turned into beef and leather. The Line picks the cotton the machines miss. It works five days a week, except when it is raining or so cold that a man's fingers can't work a hoe or a pistol. The work day is only six or seven hours and the pace isn't very difficult, but most of the convicts are from urban areas and for them farm work is depressingly dull. Most men assigned to the Line hate it.

A man newly arrived at Ellis or coming back on a new sentence or parole violation, unless he has a demonstrable physical ailment or a needed skill, is usually assigned to the Line for several months. Few stay in the Line very long. Most move to building and factory jobs or get into training programs. But there are some for whom the Line is forever. There are men who prefer the Line because they like field labor, but they are rare. Most men in the Ellis Line are there because they are constantly in and out of trouble or because they can't convince the Classification Board that they would stay out of trouble if they were given another job. And the threat of being returned to the Line is what keeps many other Texas convicts with nice jobs or school assignments behaving well.

After the men from the Line return to the prison in the evening, take off their clothes, and are searched, they move to the shower room, bathe immediately, and are given fresh clothing, all of which is identical: white cotton jackets, white cotton trousers. "It makes them less likely to fall out in the heat," a field officer says. "It makes us better targets if we try to run," a convict says.

After dressing, the men go to their cellblocks to await the call-out for dinner. Before entering their cells they are searched again. After meals, they are searched one more time. If they go to an evening activity—church, Alcoholics Anonymous, shop, the gym, a class—they are searched on the way back. Sometimes they are searched just passing from one part of the hall to another.

During the day and through the night there are counts, which let the guards and captains and wardens know whether or not order continues to reign in their world. At count time, things freeze. Cell doors are closed. Guards walk the concrete paths in front of the tiers of cells, mumbling numbers, writing on a clipboard or a pad. When they're finished they take slips of paper to a desk in the middle of the long hall, where the building officer on duty waits and tallies.

The slips come in from all the wings, from the job locations outside, from isolation, from Death Row. The slips tell how many men are on bench warrants, how many are in the hospital or on emergency reprieve for a family funeral, how many departed today for good, and how many are newly arrived.

When the building officer's tally is completed, it is compared to what it is supposed to be—the number officially in the prison. If there is a discrepancy, the error is chased down. Errors are rare at Ellis. When the count is done, activities resume. Officers relax. Doors open and close. The count slips are taken to the building major's office, where they are recorded and put away.

What this life on the Line is for Ellis, Ellis is for the Texas prison system as a whole. If an inmate at another prison gets into minor trouble, he might lose his job in the building or shop and wind up picking cotton or keeping the turnip patch clean. But if he gets into big trouble—hurts somebody, runs off, gets caught trying to smuggle in drugs or a weapon—he goes to Ellis.

Ellis keeps a lot of violence at other prisons from happening. Its reputation has nothing to do with brutality or violence; what prisoners hate and fear about Ellis is that of all the not-very-free TDC units, Ellis is the least free of all. It is thus not only an institution in which almost 2,400 men—most of them convicted of crimes of violence—are carefully controlled, but also an institution that imposes a measure of self-control on the 23,000 other men in the Texas penal system.

The Texas prison system is presently under fierce attack in federal court. The issues the U.S. Department of Justice, in *Ruiz et al. v. Estelle,* has brought before Judge William Wayne Justice include everything from illegal power exercised by inmates over other inmates to overcrowding and inadequate medical care. But what is really at issue is the degree to which the TDC controls the lives of its inmates, and the fundamental premises of the Texas prison system. Some correctional experts think it peculiar that the Justice Department should be mounting a major attack on what they consider the best prison system in the country. But TDC's critics say it isn't the best system at all—only the most efficient.

Whatever inmate power exists in Texas prisons exists only when the officials want it to. Inmate strikes, common in many states, are rare in the TDC. The wave of sit-downs marking the start of *Ruiz* lasted only a few days in the six prisons where they occurred. The strike lasted longest at Ellis—the entire Line was off work for a week, and about two hundred Line workers didn't go back to their jobs until the end of October. Few of the industrial workers joined in the strike—they had too much to lose. Fifteen years ago, prison officials would have forced the men back to work immediately, but the days of using clubs on passive resisters are gone forever. There was no violence during the October work stoppage at Ellis. The officials simply waited it out, and while they waited they made their plans for the disciplinary proceedings that would follow.

"This is Ellis," said one of the assistant wardens. "When the rules are broken, something is done about it. We're not going to do it right now, when things are so volatile. And we can't do it all at once, because there are procedures to be followed for each infraction, and it's going to take a long time. But we've got a long time."

TDC's budget last year was slightly over $56 million, and the cost would have been far greater if the convicts did not feed and clothe themselves. Prison industries supply to some state agencies a wide variety of items at prices far below what private industries would demand. Ellis has a dental lab that makes full and partial plates for convicts and inmates of many other state institutions; the most complicated set of plates costs just $90. The Ellis bus repair factory will take a Gulf Coast county's salt-rotted and kid-shredded school bus and make it better than new for $2,000 to $3,000. Actually, the counties couldn't get most of their decayed buses repaired at any price, because most body shops find they require too much space to be economical. Outside mechanics say the work done by the Ellis convicts is better than what is done in most repair shops, and the reason is the inmates have time to do a good job. Ellis also has a dairy, a cotton gin, a sawmill, and a brush factory. It produces highway signs, furniture, and inmate uniforms, shoes, boots, and belts.

"What's important is, these inmates get to do useful work that helps them and helps other people," says TDC Director W. J. Estelle, Jr. "They're not just making little rocks out of big rocks or hanging around going to seed. Some of them learn trades they can use when they get out. They get more experience in that bus barn or the dental laboratory than most free-world people ever get. And when they do get out—contrary to the folklore—there are jobs available to them."

No Texas inmates are paid money for their work, and some inmates say they should get at least a minimum wage. Others would be happy with anything. Inmates in Texas prisons are not allowed to carry cash, but they can enter their money into special accounts and withdraw it in the form of scrip with which they can buy things at the commissaries or order them from the free world. A man with a pension or regular gifts from his family can make out rather well.

Although the prisoners are not permitted by Texas law to earn money for their work, the prison does pay them in time. State-Approved Trusties (SAT)—half the inmate population—draw two-for-one good time. Every month they serve puts two months in their time accounts; a man with ten remaining years who is made an SAT serves those ten years in five calendar years. Good time earned also brings parole-eligibility dates closer. The men in the Line are in one of three grades. Lines II and III are disciplinary: Line II draws forty days for every thirty days served, and Line III draws day for day. Everyone else, even men just arriving at the Diagnostic Unit in Huntsville in custody of their county sheriffs, is Line I, which draws fifty days for every thirty served.

Texas has the most liberal good-time laws in the country, which is curious since Texas also gives the longest sentences and is the most reluctant to grant parole. The prison system bears the burden of the courts' prodigality and the parole board's parsimony. Texas prisons now hold 25,000 inmates, more than any other state prison, an increase of 50 per cent in only four years. Ellis, like all other Texas prisons, is now terribly crowded.

The good-time grades are particularly important at Ellis, where there are so many men doing heavy time and so few who have much chance of being paroled. A change in grade from SAT to Line III doubles the years ahead to be served. Men with trusty jobs are very careful.

George Beto, Estelle's predecessor as TDC director and now on the faculty in the criminal justice program at Sam Houston State University, used to tell visitors that the administration of good time and the presence of the Line kept inmates working hard in school programs and behaving properly on other jobs.

"That's kind of paternalistic," I said the first time I heard him say that.

"You mean as opposed to having people self-motivate themselves to get an education and advance themselves at work?" I nodded and he shrugged. "I'm sure it is. I'm not happy with it. But do you know why most of these people are in here? Self-regulation, at least as far as society was concerned, got bypassed somewhere. This isn't a community of people who have grasped the rules."

For that reason, Ellis has a lot of rules of its own, more explicit and strict than society's. Rules direct behavior in the dining hall, walking patterns in the central corridor, length of hair, care of the cells. Rules govern everyone and everything. Violators are nailed. Petty infractions result in extra days of work, evenings spent shelling peanuts, cell restrictions. Serious infractions—fighting, possessing weapons, homosexual affairs, mutiny—get heavier punishments: as much as two weeks in solitary, loss of accumulated good time, reduction in grade, assignment to the Line.

Each night, the men who were written up that day for infractions stand against the wall in the corridor near an official's office. One by one they are called in and formally notified of the charges against them. Some plead guilty immediately; those who don't have hearings later. The members of the disciplinary committees are rotated to minimize the likelihood of prejudicial dispositions being given to regular offenders because of personality conflicts.

At one recent disciplinary session, the committee included the supervisor of the bus factory, one of the psychologists, and a field captain.

The first man was charged with working slowly in the fields. He said he had been working well and that he was written up only because he was the last man up the ladder to dump his sack in the cotton wagon. "Someone has to be last going up that ladder unless two of us go up holding hands." The committee was not amused; he was given five days of extra work. "That's fair," he said bitterly, "that's really fair. No matter how hard I work, I still get the same thing." The captain said the cotton wagon had been filled a dozen times that day, but no one else in the cotton squads had been written up. "I don't know about that," the inmate said, "but I think that officer has it in for me."

The second man, from the garden squad, was also charged with working slowly. "What's the problem," the captain asked, "you slower than everyone else?"

"No. But they all go faster than I do."

"That's what I said," the captain replied. The committee again gave five days of extra work.

A third man was brought in on the same charge. He said he had trouble with his glasses: they kept falling off. "That's true," the captain said. "I saw him picking them up several times." The charge was dismissed.

A fourth man in clean building whites came in and stood before the desk.

"It says here that the guard looked into your ventilation screen and saw your cellmate on your lap and he didn't have his pants on. What do you have to say about that?"

"That wasn't what happened at all. The officer was mistaken."

"What did happen?"

"We was just talking."

"With him on your lap?"

"He wasn't on my lap. It maybe just looked that way. We was talking low because it was about something private and we didn't want to disturb anybody."

"Why did the officer say he was in your lap with his pants off?"

"He was mistaken. Maybe he's got it in for us."

"Do you think he's got it in for you?"

"I didn't think so."

"So how do you plead?"

"Not guilty. I haven't done anything wrong."

"All right. Go on back. You'll be notified when we have the trial. You can call any witnesses you wish on your behalf. Do you have any witness you will want to call?"

"Yes."

"Who?"

"I don't know yet."

The man left and his cellmate came in. He stood in the same spot. The charge was read again, and the captain said, "What do you have to say about that?"

"Ain't nothing to say."

"What does that mean?"

"Means there ain't nothing to say."

"Were you sitting in his lap with your pants off?"

"Sure I was. That officer caught us."

"Why were you sitting in his lap with your pants off?"

"Why do you think?"

"So how do you plead?"

"Guilty."

Except for serious cases—which don't happen often at Ellis—disciplinary hearings like this aren't like criminal trials in the free world. The usual assumption is that the charge is legitimate and the facts are not in serious dispute. One convict complained, "They always believe the guards. A convict doesn't stand a chance."

A major said, "So who should we believe? The inmates? If I have reason to think a guard is wrong—and that sometimes happens—I'll say so. Sometimes I'll tear it up without even having a hearing. But if I have no reason to think the guard is wrong or to disbelieve him, then I accept his word. Otherwise, this place falls apart."

"It's a mistake to look at those minor disciplinaries as trials," George Beto says. "They're like coming before a magistrate when you've been caught by a DPS radar setup. They're disposition hearings, that's all."

In earlier years, Texas officials didn't bother with formal hearings for anything. If a man was thought to be working too slowly, he would be put on the ground and beaten with the "bat," a strip of leather 24 inches long and 4 inches wide attached to a foot-long wooden handle. "When the bat would leave, the skin would leave with it," one man, who still bore the scars, told me when I first visited Ellis fifteen years ago. Convicts who got into trouble in the building might spend a night handcuffed to the bars—with their feet off the floor.

Texas then probably had the most miserable prisons in the country. Many of the guards were nasty, the buildings were awful, the work was killing, and the convicts were badly fed, sick, terrified, and mean. Escape attempts were common, and so were self-mutilations, particularly cutting of the Achilles tendon to keep from having to work. You could tell the men who had cut their ankles because their feet flopped in a peculiar way when they walked.

The major changes came in the fifties and sixties. State money began seeping into the prison system. Convicts were no longer tortured or leased out to wealthy landowners. The official name was changed from the Texas Prison System to the Texas Department of Corrections, and the change was more than cosmetic. O. B. Ellis (the prison's namesake) was hired from Shelby County, Tennessee, and he began many of the changes, most notably, the enormous construction program. When Ellis died in 1961, George Beto, an ex-president of Concordia Lutheran College in Austin and former member of the prison board, was persuaded to come back from Concordia Seminary in Illinois to succeed Ellis. Beto retired in 1972 and was followed by Estelle, who had worked for eighteen years in the California prison system before being named warden of the Montana prisons in 1970.

The Texas Department of Corrections has a tendency to keep its innovations hidden under a bushel. TDC officials initiated industrial operations more sophisticated than similar prison programs in the industrial North. They also developed the first prison school system set up as a free nonterritorial independent school district (which means the educational program is handled by school, rather than prison, officials and is eligible for nonprison funding). And the TDC college program had an enrollment larger than that of all the other 49 state prisons combined. But if you ask prison officials what their job is, they will proudly tell you that it is to keep a lot of people locked up safely. Ask Estelle what the greatest differences are between California and Texas prisons, and the first thing he will talk about are assaults and deaths. "In four years, California had sixty-six inmate murders. In Texas we had only four. It's not that we get nicer prisoners here. I don't think that because a man gets sent to prison he should be in more danger than he is in Houston or Dallas. That's not right. Ellis has a lower homicide rate than any maximum-security prison in any of the industrial states, and it's safer than any major city in the United States."

Ellis is populated by failures in crime, and crime is a lousy business to fail in. There are very few successful criminals and you seldom find them in prison. When they are in prison, they don't stay very long. Few men in Ellis—or in TDC as a whole—got there via one-time nonviolent offenses. Texas is a law-and-order state and it has courts that hand out long sentences (for a while, Dallas courts were sending men down with 2,500- and 5,000-year maximums), but it is hard to get sent away for the first time out for anything but murder. Only one-third of the admissions each year have been in TDC before, but most have had serious encounters with the law previously. Almost everyone in Ellis has already been in prison. The men at Ellis have flunked at crime *and* at being a convict more often and more egregiously than other TDC convicts.

In the Ellis corridor one day, Harry, an old man about to go out for his sixth time, told me he always successfully beat the prosecutors when they wanted to hit him with the habitual criminal act, which carries a mandatory life sentence. "I cop out, that's what I do. Every time. I beat 'em every time on the bitch." Every time Harry is arrested for burglary or robbery, the DA threatens to prosecute for the crime and for the habitual, but he says that if Harry will confess and save the county the cost of a trial, he will get the judge to sentence Harry only to the maximum for the theft. Harry agrees every time, and he thinks he has put something over on the DA. He still considers his most recent twelve-year sentence an achievement.

Another convict told me that this is his third time in TDC, his second time at Ellis. "You got to be crazy to keep coming back here," I said.

"Yeah," he said. "I hate it here. I got my case on appeal and there's a good chance I'll get out."

"What will you do if you get out?"

He smiled, shrugged, fluttered his enormous hands. "I'll get messed up and come back here. That's what I always do. Mess up and come on back down here. This is the only place I don't get messed up."

I have come to the conclusion that what prisons do best is teach people how to be adequate prisoners. Almost everything I know about the prisons—the best and the worst of them—is awful, but that is perhaps the single most awful thing. It is one reason why men serving long sentences tend to have worse recidivism records than men serving short sentences: it is not just that long-termers are worse human beings to begin with, but that years of institutionalized life have made them unfit for the free world. A person who has adjusted perfectly to a prison—an Ellis or an Attica, though the adjustments to those two places are different—is almost always a maladjusted freak out here. I've known men who got out and committed crimes absolutely guaranteed to fail, so they could come home to prison with a measure of honor intact. A person can't say, "I came back because I can't handle the choices out there" or "I came back because this is the only place I feel safe." But he can say, "I got caught with a smoking .357 in my hand."

Ellis maintains a potential mass of violence at an amazingly safe level. It also maintains a level of depression and woe at an equally astoundingly safe level. Prison officials are proud that the convicts aren't killing one another out there; I'm amazed that the convicts aren't killing themselves. To think seriously of spending fifteen or twenty years in the sparkling and orderly quiet of Ellis could, as John Berryman once put it, "curry disorder in the finest brain." The way to survive Ellis is by not thinking of such things.

Ellis is a warehouse for almost 2,400 men, some of whom have done terrible things, but its long corridor is the safest avenue you will ever walk in the deep dark of night. The price of that safety is high, and everyone at Ellis—keepers and kept alike—is constantly aware of how much that safety costs. The officials would prefer to do it some other way, but no one has yet designed another way that works.

"Ellis isn't like any other prison in TDC," George Beto once said to me.

"What's different about it?" I asked.

He paused a long time, skipping the obvious things. "Ellis is the end of the line."

Finding the Topknot

(*Anonym,* 1970)

When I first met Sam, the man whose release from the penitentiary provided the occasion for this essay, he was midway in a five-year prison term for burglary. He'd done time once before: two years for forging checks. He liked forging checks but became too well known, so he shifted to burglary, an occupation in which there were only accidental confrontations with the victims. Sam's discussions of safecracking and check writing as trades, along with comments by other crooks, police, and lawyers, form the basis of *A Thief's Primer* (Jackson 1972). A much-abbreviated version of this essay forms part of the postscript to that book.

IT IS ALWAYS GOOD to have along for the ride someone who knows the scene and gambits. You save time. When I drove into Huntsville, Kid, who once was a pretty fair safecracker and very strung-out dope addict, said, "Try the bus station first. He'll probably be there in case we don't show up."

"I told him I'd pick him up at the prison,".I said.

"There's only one bus in the afternoon to Houston, so we usually wait for our rides at the Greyhound depot. If they don't show we can get the bus out. Otherwise we're stuck here four extra hours. People who pick up people like us sometimes don't show up."

We found Sam in the bus station waiting room. He was looking at the pictures in a magazine and didn't see us until we called his name.

On the way down, Sam beamed and gleamed and Kid did a lot of the talking. He told us he'd been on cough syrup for a while since he'd been out but now was off and pretty much straight. Sam and I both nodded like it was news, but we'd both heard rumors from other sources that Kid had knocked off a couple of drugstores and had scored for some doctor's bags a few months back. And he'd been seen in Houston with a character named Alvin with whom he had nothing in common but dope. "If he's with that jerk," I'd been told, "he's got to be on something. Why else would anybody talk to Alvin."

We stopped at a small quonset bar off Interstate 45 so Sam could have a first beer. I played the pinball machine while he and Kid shot a game of pool. Kid asked Sam if he had a job lined up and Sam shrugged the question away. "You get used to it," Kid said. Sam didn't say anything. Aretha Franklin sang out of the jukebox, amazing the air in the corrugated iron.

We got back in the car and continued south. Kid talked about his job, his new wife, making it. Sam shrugged again.

"I just like to party," Sam said. And, a little later: "A lot of people *like* it. I'm *hooked* on it. I just don't want to get up with any hangover and go to work. I want to stay in bed if that's the way I feel. And I don't like responsibilities."

We turn along Westheimer and Sam gets very excited when he spots a joint he made once. "I don't know why," he says, and after a while I realize that that was the concluding sentence of the previous discussion. We pass some more places he remembers. "Maybe it's a sense of resentment because they make it. I watch them from across the street and hope they have a good day. Today it's his, tonight it's mine."

Down a street lined with glistening new shops, all metal and angles. Sam stares at them. "Boy, if they had been here five years ago we'd have had a relationship."

"Hard," Kid says, "they're all floodlit inside."

"You can get around that. What kinda boxes they got in those places?"

"Tin cans."

"I don't like tin cans. I like *real* boxes, man. On tin cans you can cut your fingers."

Driving on. We talk more about safes: good scores and bad scores, safes he'd peeled or punched or ripped or blown or couldn't touch at all, and finally he says what I suspect he's really wanted to say all afternoon: "I just dig stealing. I *like* it."

We picked up Kid's new wife, then went to Gaito's and had dinner with wine. Sam didn't usually drink wine, but tonight was special. Afterwards, we dropped off Kid and his wife and took off for something else.

Along the back roads of the sparsely inhabited outskirts of Houston we looked for a country bar where Sam was to deliver a message to the girlfriend of a man still in prison. We went back and forth across old U.S. 75 on one empty road after the other, we asked directions and were given them and used them up till we found how bad they were and then asked again and got more bad directions. At one small filling station—some off-brand I'd never heard of—we met a fortyish ex-con named Grin who recognized Sam and smiled at us toothlessly and shivered inside a beat-up oversize army field jacket. Grin didn't like the job but it was better than jail he said. He didn't say why or how. He gave Sam two packs of cigarettes as a present and carefully repeated his directions to the country bar.

Grin's directions weren't any good either. We drove.

Finally, fifty or a hundred miles after dinner, we found the place and realized we'd started out in the wrong direction from the beginning, for we were now on the far side of town near U.S. 59.

"It don't matter," Sam said "For this kind of woman you don't want to be on time anyway because they don't respect you for it." I looked at my watch: we were nearly two hours late.

A woman was getting out of an old car as we were pulling into the partially gravelled parking lot. Her breath made visible puffs before her face as she went up the steps to the bar. Inside we found out she was the woman we were looking for. The joint was no warmer than outside, the only difference was there was no wind. Few places down there were ready for the rare cold snaps and this wasn't one of them.

The girl's name was Harriet and she bore too much makeup on a hatchety face and under her coat she wore a bright purple sweater. She told us she worked as a B-girl in a downtown stripjoint and made $400 a week, most of it from commissions on hustling drinks.

It was a small square building with four tables, a short straight bar, a pool table dominated by one man at least 40 years old who wore a Texas A&M sweatshirt, a jukebox, and a stripper who performed for three 45 rpm singles every thirty minutes. The stripper was a pretty blonde with a sad piquant mouth that didn't go very well with the rest of her face which wasn't very sad or very much of anything. The expression didn't change; it was cast or frozen. When she came away from the end of the bar to do her bit she wore a bright satin robe that came off right away. At first you could see the goosebumps but then she got moving fast and sweating some and the bumps went away. By the middle of the second record of each set she got down to pasties and panties. At the beginning of the third 45 record she swung her pastied breasts one at a time, and for a finale got them going in opposite directions simultaneously. Her mouth kept not quite smiling.

When the girl finished her set Harriet left the table and Sam said, "She drove up in that 1955 Ford. Four hundred a week my ass."

Harriet came back from the can and complained about the owner, an attractive woman who looked 30 but who Harriet insisted was 38 and maybe even 39. We were told that the owner had had silicone injections but didn't massage herself as the doctor had instructed and now suffered from an embarrassing lumpiness. "Me," Harriet said, "I'm just a 32-C but I'm proud of it." Harriet puffed out her pride. "You come to the joint where I work and you can tell which ones have used that shit. Their tits stick straight out."

The night eroded in talk and beer. I hate beer in the cold and sometime in there I turned away from the conversation. After a while Harriet must have worn out because Sam said, "Let's go," and we went, leaving her there alone at the table while the middle-aged man in his college sweatshirt continued to burn up the pool table.

The next night we left Houston, heading out on Texas 35. We passed Ramsey, Retrieve and some of the other prison farms, through Bay City and into Palacios. When we passed the jail Sam said, "I remember one time in there, the Rangers were beating the shit out of me and the sheriff said, 'Cut it out.' And, man, I just *loved* that guy. But then he said, 'Cut it out. If you have to do that take him out in the country and do it.' The last thing in the world I wanted at that moment was that nice country air!"

The road was black and shining in the dark and we passed and sometimes ran over already squashed cadavers of large birds. Sometimes ducks with what seemed broken legs tried to scurry out of the headlights and Sam told me that in the night they often mistook the blackness of the road for quiet water and zoomed in to a big surprise.

Then through Port Lavaca and to the last curve after which we could see ahead the night lights of Corpus Christi. On either side of the road were the black skeletons of drilling rigs silhouetted against the dark blue sky. Sam told me about working in the fields, about how you move a rig when a hole is no good, how his uncle lost a fortune once when a rig was wrecked on him, how his father died moving one out the Valley.

We were going to find some friends of his and spend the night there in Corpus. I checked into a motel and then we went to see Sam's mother. The house was on a quiet dark street where few lights burned. She sat in a chair in the bedroom, a tight little space that was crowded with just the three of us in there. Except for the bathroom this was the only room with a heater in it. She didn't say much and the conversation was very formal. I started to leave but they both insisted I stay, as if it would be even more difficult without a stranger there because then there wouldn't even be an excuse for the formalities. She told him that now that he was out of the prison hospital he could stop taking the pills the doctors had given him and he would be all right. He told her he was dying of blood cancer and if he stopped taking the pills he wouldn't be able to do anything at all. She didn't want to talk about it further and the subject hung there like a stink and got in the way of any other conversation, even the formalities.

Sam had been hoping the family would offer him enough money to go to Lahey Clinic in Boston or Mayo Clinic, but if she wouldn't admit he was sick she wasn't about to part with any money to have him treated.

So we left pretty soon.

The streets were cold and empty. We drove from joint to joint, looking for people, for characters. But there wasn't anyone. No one at all. Just strangers. We went into a go-go joint where the dancer was an incredibly ugly brunette with a massive beehive hairdo and green satin pajamas. It was a new place and Sam saw no old faces. We couldn't even find some of the joints he remembered well. One was a pool hall, smelling of fresh varnish, empty but for the manager and the hustler. A warehouse he'd once burgled was gone, leaving a weed-littered lot. The old all-night eatery, Nixon's, was closed when we went by at midnight. Characters Sam knew from the joint weren't where he expected them to be and people he knew from before he went down weren't anywhere at all.

In the Negro section we sought a barbecue joint Sam remembered as serving pretty good food. The barbecue joint was boarded up. There was a large bar next door and we went in. About five people were there: the fat friendly woman who ran the place, an idiot assistant, and a few customers. The jukebox was nice, full of Otis Redding and B. B. King and other things. On the wall were three deer heads and two Jax Beer signs. The Jax signs featured very light Negroes who drank beer while others smiled down on us. Sam talked with the fat woman about some whores he knew and the old man who had run the barbecue. The old man was dead, the whores in California. It was too cold to sit there and drink so we didn't stay very long.

As I backed the car out of the lot Sam looked up and down the empty street. A cruising car slowed down and Sam at first thought it was someone who recognized him but the driver only said, "You guys looking for some action?" We told him we weren't and he drove on away, picking up speed.

"I once couldn't walk down this street without fifteen niggers calling my name," Sam said.

No one called and we went somewhere else.

We asked for people. We hear that this one is out of town, this one hasn't been seen for a long time (How long? A *long* time.) This one is dead or maybe dead, this one is at Letty's joint (but we'd been there and the place is empty). Sam concludes that unlisted telephone numbers are the thing among the criminal element, the characters, that's why he can't find anyone. He concludes that it's the cold, that everyone is staying home, that's why he can't find anyone. That's why, that's why, that's why. The reasons continue, but they don't help very much.

We tire of beer. In Texas you can get beer and setups in public bars, for mixed drinks you have to go to a private club. We get a bottle and go to a bar but the waitress tells Sam to put the bottle away. "Don't tell me this is a private club now?"

"Hell, no. But we don't allow bottles brought in here. You just order what you want." Behind the bar is a long row of liquor bottles, like any bar up North. One assumes the management pays off well.

"Who owns this place?" Sam asks the girl.

"Why you want to know?"

He tells her the name of a friend of his who owned it when he was last there. She relaxes a little. "He left town a couple of years ago." She tells us the name of the man who now owns it and goes to get our drinks.

"Christ," Sam says, "I know that sonofabitch. I stole his wife off a him once."

"Stole?"

"She was a pulled-up whore when they got married and then she decided she didn't want to be pulled up any more and come to see me and I put her back to work."

"What did he do?"

"What *could* he do. He's nothing. And that's what he did. Nothing." Sam looked around the bar. The piano player played his piano. The waitress hovered near another table. A few men sat at the bar. Someone came in through the back, from the kitchen. "That's him right there. Hasn't changed at all."

"Let's split."

"Why you want to do that?"

"Man, you're just out of the joint. You can't afford a fight. And I'm not particularly interested in one."

"Nothing to worry about. He had his chance back then and didn't pick it up. I faced him down and didn't even have a gun on me. If he didn't do anything then he's not going to do anything now."

Sam's chair scraped back. "Where are you going?" I said.

"See if he knows where anybody is."

Sam walked to the bar and said something to the man. The man shook his head. Sam said something else but the man shook his head again, and again. Sam returned to our table, walking stiffly.

"Let's get out of here. Now," he said.

"What about the drinks?"

"Ahh. I said let's go." His face was a bad color.

As we went out the door the man called, "Y'all come back now," the way they do down there.

It was still as cold as before. Sam didn't say anything as I started the motor.

"What's the matter?" I said. "What did he say to you?"

"Nothing."

"What do you mean?"

"Nothing. He didn't say nothing at all. Just that he didn't know where Eddie the Fish was. Or Two-Shoes. Or Lola. Or Tommy Sunday."

"So? Why you so bugged?"

"He didn't remember me!"

Which did it for Corpus. It was cold death, creeping, sitting, waiting, walking, everyplace.

Anybody who's ever lived west of Beaumont and south of Dallas knows there's only one thing to do when everything gets too hairy and grim for comfort: "Let's go to Mexico," I said.

"Yeah. That's what we ought to do. Let's go to Mexico."

I checked out of the motel room I hadn't used and we were on the road again, still heading southwest, this time on Texas 44 through Alice where Sam had once spent all night on a safe that he couldn't even scratch ("And I never did get it. It never did give. If it gave a sixteenth of an inch I could get it, but I never could get a sixteenth of an inch.") to Freer in Duval County where we picked up U.S. 59 and a lot more speed. About then he made his only comment on the Corpus wreckage.

"It's a hell of a thing to leave there being somebody, one of the in people, and come back after five years and you don't know nobody and nobody knows you. Not even your own family. A hell of a thing."

In the moonlight there was nothing but mesquite and rabbits (coming back, later, I found there was nothing but mesquite and rabbits in the daylight either). Sixty-five miles straight down to the Mexican border.

We registered at the Holiday Inn in Laredo and drove across the border for a look-around, intending to come back and get some sleep.

Sam wanted to show me some joint in Boys' Town, but when we got to where it was supposed to be there was nothing but water-troughed muddy streets and dark silent houses. One massive whorehouse on the main road had been converted into a garish gift shop with big things hanging from everyplace one might hang a big thing. It was cold and dark and alone and like Corpus all over again.

A boy rattled down the street on a bike, seeming perfectly natural in the 3 A.M. chill and we stopped him to ask what happened to Boys' Town. "They move it," he said. "You go down here 14 blocks and then turn left, then you go ten blocks and you see it on your right." He pedaled off.

"What are you waiting for?" Sam said. "Let's go."

"I can't think of any town in the world somebody could stop me in and I could rattle off just like that the number of blocks from wherever I was to someplace 25 blocks away."

"He probably gets asked a lot. Let's go."

We went, and when we got to the place at the end of the ten-block run we saw off to the right some lights. There seemed nothing but fields between. We wandered a while and found a dirt road pocked with deep holes. We came out the other end in front of a walled enclave painted some pastel color. At the entrance were some police who didn't pay any attention to us.

Inside, one street made a loop and there were buildings on either side of it, two concentric rectangles of bars and whorehouses. Maybe a half-dozen cars. We went in one joint and found about a dozen men and two girls. We sat at a nearby table and learned that one of the girls was an American down with her date. We had a beer, then went to another place.

A fat man talked in Spanish with the bartender. The bartender asked if we wanted a beer. Sam said he did. I said, "None for me."

"None for you?" the bartender said.

"None for me."

He returned a moment later with the two beers and set them in front of us. The fat man came over and talked about how terrible the cold was for business. His name was Topknot and he looked like Sidney Greenstreet. I had heard of him and Sam reckoned he had once met him long back. Topknot was looking for an American to handle the dice action because if a Mexican ran it the gringos wouldn't bet. Topknot knew of Sam and said he'd heard Sam had been away, which subject was immediately dropped by both. Topknot wondered if Sam would be interested in the dice action. Sam said it might be of some interest. Topknot ordered a bottle of cognac and the bartender poured unhappily because it was for free.

And it was there we wrapped it up after I don't remember exactly how long in motion, as the only window in the place that was not painted or boarded over went from nighttime back to dark morning blue. It was cold, cold as I can remember there, and in Mexico they are less prepared for cold than Houston.

The bartender kept giving us phony Pedro Domencq, which puzzled me because you'd expect people at least to confine booze counterfeiting to something potable in the original, and in between fiddling with the large brown butane space heater that never, for all his fiddling, threw out one perceivable calorie of warmth.

The blue went gray as we sat there in that frozen whorehouse bar in Nuevo Laredo talking over big scores and high rollers with Topknot. The bartender rounded the table again with the Pedro Domencq surrogate. It didn't warm.

High rollers and old times.

Sam told about a character who took him to L.A. on a plane and when they were there had a tailor come to the room to fit them both. They got six suits, all of which were put on the hotel bill. The man gave Sam $500 and told him to take a walk for a few hours. When Sam returned, the man had $16,000 from selling insurance stock. He wrote a check to cover their hotel bill, then left, driving a rented car. They stopped off in Vegas where he lost the entire $16,000.

Topknot told about Johnny Pango, a gambler and pimp he and Sam knew, who had come to him in an outrage one morning. Two Mexican hoods had gotten a whore of his and forced her to perform certain styles of tricks she didn't normally do. Topknot, who lived on the American side of the border, said, "So what you want *me* to do? Do that to *them?*"

"Great!" Johnny said. "Here's $500. You do what you can do and I'll double it later."

Topknot called Mexican police and in 25 minutes the two were in jail. He paid the cops $20 for the service. And in the jail the head strauss had the two treated as they had treated the girl. That was for free.

The bartender put the bottle down and again fiddled with the space heater and made us move our chairs to get where the heat was; it wasn't. He asked us if we wanted any girls. We looked at him like he was crazy: it was freezing and we were *talking*. "I don't," I said, "maybe he does." The bartender went out without asking Sam the question.

He came back a few minutes later and said, "She's getting up."

We drank and talked. A while later Topknot said, "This man is my guest. What happened to the girl?"

The bartender went out again and was gone for ten minutes. "She's too drunk to get up," he said. Sam didn't seem to mind. He was happy talking over the high rollers with Topknot.

The grey window showed streaks of rain. The day carried no warmth. Nothing did. About 7 A.M. some women came in. I won't try to describe most of them: there is nothing in the world quite like the 7 A.M. shift in a Mexican border whorehouse.

Two homed in like missiles on our table. The taller one was faster and she saw that Sam and Topknot were talking and obviously perceived that it would not do to interrupt Topknot at any time so she took the one remaining chair at the table and placed it quietly next to Sam and in a fashion I can describe only as demurely sat there, hands in lap, waiting.

The short one, who seemed made of balloons of different sizes—one large round one for her pelvis, a slightly elongated one for her trunk, two matching ones for her breasts, one too round and too large for her head (Where was the one for the neck? Good grief: no neck.)—and several plump ovals that were arms and legs, came a few steps behind and her face showed puzzlement as she tried to decide where to sit. The tall thin gringo in talk with Topknot, that must be the one with the money because otherwise why would Topknot be in such talk with him? But already the first girl was there and if she sat there too the first girl might make a scene and Topknot would not like that. But there was no chair by the other American and to drag a chair over would be to make another kind of interruption.

Her small round eyes switched back and forth and she neared the table, then somewhere inside the round head she decided and the eyes locked. I was leaning on the table, so she took the only available seat: the brown space heater, directly behind me, and perhaps she was finally the only one of us close enough to draw any heat from it.

She sat quietly for a moment, then I heard movement and felt the two matched balloons bopping into my back. Bopping. I sat there. The balloon of her head appeared next to mine and just below her mustache her mouth said, "You like me, right?"

I drank the last of my phony Pedro Domencq, which just then seemed extremely important.

"You like me, right?" I shrugged. "Come on," she said. "Let's go."

"No."

"Why not? You like me, right?" She moved her hands. I saw my glass was empty.

"No."

"Why no?"

"I don't feel like it."

"I don't understand English. You like me? Come on." Her hands moved more.

"No."

"Hey, you ——?" She said a word I didn't know and didn't catch, but Topknot did because he looked up and laughed.

"What did she say?" I said.

"She wants to know if you're queer."

"No, I just . . . "

"No?" she said, smiling, then making an O with her mouth inside the O of her head. "Then you like me. Come on."

I got up and she beamed, balloons on balloons in balloons around balloons. I walked to the nearest table and took one of the chairs and brought it back and set it right next to the thin girl. I pointed at it and said, "You."

The balloon girl frowned, pouted, raised her eyebrows, moved parts, then shrugged. She said the word for queer again. Topknot said to her, "No," and then went on in Spanish, explaining I wasn't interested.

She sat there a little curved and I felt a little sad. It must be hell to be on the 7 A.M. shift. You know who gets that shift. But I wasn't that sad.

Sam and Topknot ignored us all; they had another bottle of cognac between them, half gone now, and the words were still of old scores, great games, and someplace else where the women were polished and the action fast and the money big and the air like crystal.

I went outside and sloshed through the muddy street to the car, drove for a while, crossed the border to Laredo and went to the motel to shower and change clothes. In the room were two steak and egg breakfasts, still hot, that Sam had pre-ordered the night before. That meant it was now about 10 A.M. I ate all of one and part of the other, realizing we'd been drinking and driving and talking a lot but hadn't eaten for a long time.

Back across the border. I walked the downtown streets and shopped for presents. When I went back to Boys' Town it was starting to come alive. A man drove up to the entrance ahead of me in an old Ford. Inside were three children and a woman. The woman got out and the man drove back to town with the kids. Whores were parading in front of the hairdresser's shop. There were a few dry spots above the large deep-tracked mudholes.

I didn't see Sam anywhere. Topknot's place was empty, except for another bartender who didn't know anything. I wondered if Sam had gotten into a switch with Topknot. If he had, there was no telling where he was or what condition he might be in.

A street sweeper (I think that's what he was: he was dressed like one and he carried one of those enormous brooms they have, but there weren't any sidewalks or pavement there and I don't know what he did with his enormous broom) waved me down.

"I'm looking for an American without a car, a tall thin guy," I said.

"You mean the gringo in the sweater?"

"Yes."

"He's over there."

He pointed and I saw Sam, stumbling through the muddy street, alone and stoned but apparently undamaged. "Thanks," I said.

"That's 25 cents."

"What?"

"25 cents. My tip."

I gave him the quarter and swung the car to where Sam tried to find places where the mud wasn't deeper than his Stacey Adams.

"Man," he said when he got into the car, "I have never been so boxed." He said that three times, then asked me to stop at a certain place not far down the street. I asked him why. "I've got to talk with this waitress a minute."

I park the car and we go into the joint. It is morning and there is no one there but the bartender. Sam orders a beer. I tell him we have to leave because I have to be three hundred miles up the road by nighttime and that checkout time in the Laredo motel is noon.

"Hell, let's pay for another day. Let's stay another day, man."

"I can't. I've got work to do."

"Lemme see this broad first."

The bartender brings Sam his beer. Sam asks where the girl is and the man points to one of the cribs out back. "Drink the beer while I'm gone," he says. He walks toward the crib. I see him talking with a girl in green slacks. He returns shortly and says, "Let's go."

"Aren't you going to drink your beer?"

"No."

We get in the car and he tells me about another joint he found which he says is fabulous. I tell him we haven't time to visit it. More people are moving around the street now. Another car drives up with a man behind the wheel and some children in back and a woman in front beside the man, and like the other car, the woman gets out and the man drives away.

"But man," Sam says, "we had it to ourselves for awhile, didn't we now." I say we did and he says, "Man, am I boxed. I told that last whore. . . . He mumbles off into something I can only make out parts of.

I drive to the border. Just before he passes out Sam says, missing some syllables, "We *did* have it to ourselves didn't we."

I agree and we are waved through Customs and are home again in Texas.

It's Just Petty Violence, Sir

(*Buffalo Spree,* 1985)

I grew up in the Fort Greene and Bedford-Stuyvesant sections of Brooklyn and I've spent much of my professional time as a social scientist and journalist in places where violence is an immediate possibility. Like most people who have grown up and worked extensively in such places, I've learned to carry myself a certain way on the street and in unfamiliar places. It's not so much paranoia as a condition of readiness, an inability ever to relax completely.

It's supposed to be different at home. Home is where you go to relax completely, the place you don't have to wonder about movements in the shadows, or sounds in another room. This piece is about a minor incident in which I learned that my assumption of simple geographical safety was simplistic, even naive.

The dog who impresses the policemen and goes berserk in honor of the mailman in this piece was a Samoyed named Jerusalem, not the fyce named Lulu who bit the congressman I told you about in "The Battle of the Pentagon."

THAT MORNING, I WAS reading the manuscript of a friend's new book. Diane had fallen asleep on the other end of the couch, a half-graded term paper in her lap, the pen still in her hand. The dog was curled up like a white pelt under the coffee table. The first birds had begun to chatter, which meant dawn was no more than an hour off.

My favorite time of day. The light changes rapidly and the air is almost always clear. Even before I am aware of the shift from black of night to deep blue of approaching dawn I can discern silhouettes of buildings and trees where only moments before there was only uniform darkness. Gradually, in the coming hour, the yellow light of the reading lamp would merge with and then be bleached out by the cooler light of day. It was time to open the curtains.

Before I had the chance to let in the morning light, reality came crashing through the windows. More accurately, the windows came crashing into the room.

Ours is one of those large elegant Buffalo houses built before the graduated income tax made such places improbable. When we bought it a decade ago the suburban Amherst school systems still had the reputation of being far better than Buffalo schools, so middle-class couples with young children and not a great deal of money for or interest in private schools tended to settle in the white suburbs. That meant people like us—working professionals—could get these wonderful city houses for very little money. Before the energy crisis, these houses were fabulous bargains.

The ground floor of our house has French windows all around. Each window is composed of two doors, each with a pane of thick glass five feet high and two feet wide. Above each double door is a semicircular pane. Six of the large windows face the street. One reason we bought the house was the excellent light.

There were, in succession too fast to count, several thuds accompanied and followed by the sharp crystal sound of falling glass. A curtain at the far end of the room puffed out a few feet, then fluttered back like the slow-motion scenes in corny television shows. The curtain didn't quite regain the perpendicular. A floor lamp to my right teetered as if it were making up its mind, then crashed across a glass table and rolled lazily to the floor. I had a curious sensation of being in galloping and frozen time at once.

Diane sat straight up. "What's going on?" she said, still half asleep.

"Someone's shooting out our goddamned windows."

She jumped up to look and before I could tell her to stay down she tore a long bloody cut in her thigh on the shiny corner of our chrome-framed leather couch. She sat back down and looked at the blood and I wondered just what we were supposed to do now.

We had been back in Buffalo only two days after a month-long car trip across the country with a lot of film equipment and the dog. Both of us regularly fly a great deal and, like many Americans, we had become used to consuming enormous distances in little bits of time. We had decided we would spend time on this trip experiencing those lost distances. The day we'd left the city had been nearly immobilized by one of those early spring blizzards. From the time we got on the Thruway to the Pennsylvania border our only reference point in the world outside our car were the flickering taillights of a huge P.I.E. semi. Then things got better.

We filmed part of a documentary in San Francisco, then visited a friend shooting a big-budget movie in Las Vegas and had silent sit-down parts as sleazy gamblers in a sleazy gambling joint. We lost a fan belt in the desert near Teec Nos Pas, Arizona, closer to nowhere than either of us had ever been stranded before, and within moments kindly strangers arrived with the necessary metric tools, patience, and skills. I cursed the perverse Volvo engineering that located the fan belt behind two other belts and I praised my long-defunct Chevrolet Six that never broke down anywhere until long after the odometer had started its second complete cycle. The strangers told us to stop worrying and stop carrying on; they said we would better spend the time enjoying the desert sunset. In a valley west of Los Alamos, Diane looked at a particularly beautiful configuration of hills and high desert and said she for the first time understood the representation aspect of Indian art, that the splendid abstract geometry was simply based on what that astringent world looked like. Going through a Colorado mountain pass the Volvo behaved badly. It slowed to fifteen miles an hour and seemed ready to begin slipping backwards as we climbed through eleven thousand feet. Then it shuddered through the top and we coasted down and regained power for a drive across a green high mountain plain eight thousand feet up in the Rockies. Only two weeks earlier I had flown over the same area with Vine Deloria, Jr., who had looked out the plane's window and said, "I had an unsettling experience around here last week. I realized that the distance a friend and I had driven in the past thirty minutes had taken the Donner party six weeks." There was a nice sense of immediate and distant and ancient history, all three present all at once.

By the Thursday we got back to Buffalo, the dunes of snow had nearly all melted and grass once again greened. A note from the house sitter said all had gone well, a casserole was in the refrigerator, Cablescope was coming Friday to run a new cable. The bags were unpacked, the mound of mail was sorted into four piles—letters, junk, bills, magazines. We read the letters, discarded the junk, left the bills and magazines alone for a while. The man from the cable company put in a new cable and we relaxed into the inanity of late-night television and the pleasure of knowing we were home; we were where if something broke we could call someone to fix it and in the meantime we had our entire normal world exactly in place, all our resources perfectly on call. And that was when the room filled with shattered glass.

Diane went up the back stairway to get the old .22 rifle from a closet. The rifle's entire experience in this world had been devoted to shooting cans a few afternoons when we had lived in California several years earlier. The bullets were somewhere else in the house. I reached for the phone, keeping out of a direct line with the windows, and dialed 911. Even though the shooters couldn't see me through the still-closed curtains, they might start firing again and they might get lucky. I gave the operator my name and address and made sure she had the facts right. I still remember the time a woman in nearby Kenmore called 911 to report someone breaking down her back door and the 911 operator had sent the assignment to the wrong police unit. By the time the right police got the message the woman had been murdered.

"Someone is shooting out my windows," I said.

"And when did the incident occur?" the operator asked. She wasn't the least bit excited.

"It just happened."

"How long ago, sir?" A slight tone of exasperation to the voice.

"Lady: someone just shot out my goddamned windows. Just now."

"Then we'll send a car to investigate."

"Thank you."

"You're welcome."

Diane came back with the rifle and told me the window in the upstairs front bathroom had also been blown out. The light had been on in that room so after she found the .22 she crawled to the light switch and reached up from the floor to turn it off. I held the rifle loosely in my left hand, just the way I'd seen someone do it in a movie. The rifle didn't seem very useful.

"Is that thing loaded?" Diane asked.

"Of course not. I wouldn't have a loaded gun in the house."

"I'm glad of that," she said, "but what do you think you're going to do with it?"

We went upstairs and lurked in the shadows of the front bedroom. Nothing seemed to move in the park across the street. There were no cars and no people about. We didn't know if the combat was over or if we'd had a mere prelude to an all-out attack. The sky was still dark and a light rain fell on the empty street. The park was a black space, full of secrets.

We decided not to wake the kids, who somehow had slept through the cacophony. If it was over, no need to terrify them; if it wasn't over, well, we'd wake them when it seemed there was a good reason for letting them in on our panic. I opened the window to get a better view.

"You should get away from that window," Diane said.

"Right you are." I stepped back into the shadows.

As she talked I moved my fingers through a bottom bureau drawer. I found the box of bullets and loaded the rifle. My fingers were not the least bit steady and I dropped two of them. I went to the window again.

"I wish you would stop doing that."

"I'm not used to loading this thing in the dark," I said, my voice slightly annoyed.

"I mean standing in front of the window."

My body had pumped out a lot of adrenalin and my brain didn't have the slightest idea what to do with it. The waiting was terrible. The bedroom clock was electric; it didn't even hum. If it had been the old-fashioned kind I might have heard the ticking and I could have known whether time was racing or crawling by.

"How long has it been now?"

"Not long," she said.

"It seems long," I said.

I dialed 911 and asked if they were sending a car or not. (What would have been my threat if they said no? That I'd take my business somewhere else?) A man with a bored voice said a car was on the way. He was probably used to people in situations like this who wanted immediate service, people who understood nothing of the realities of the world. I hung up the phone and picked up the rifle again. "This is just like the movies," I said.

"It's not like the movies at all," Diane said. "I'm never *really* scared in the movies."

Twelve minutes after the first shattered glass, the police car pulled into our driveway, its lights off. I started toward the stairs.

"You should leave that here," Diane said, pointing to the rifle I'd forgotten I was holding.

A patrolman and a lieutenant stood outside. The dog barked at them, the first time she had barked since the neighbors had come home at midnight. After I parked her in the kitchen the policemen agreed to come in. Each wore a reassuring mass of leather, chrome, and weapons. I turned the living room lights on again.

"What seems to be the problem here?" the lieutenant said. It was almost as if he had been casually cruising the neighborhood and decided all on his own to stop by and check things out. But, from his outfit, I was sure he was a desk lieutenant, pulled out of the precinct house for the call. I wondered why they hadn't sent a regular neighborhood patrol car. (I asked him later and he told me: they didn't send a neighborhood patrol car because budget cuts had knocked out most of the cops working the 12-8 shift and only two cars patrolled this whole side of the city. And both were busy just now.)

Library of Congress. She said a program officer at NEH was very annoyed at the piece and would be writing me about it. "Mad at me personally or as editor of *JAF*?" I asked. "As editor," my interlocutor said. "Fine," I said, "I'll be happy to publish the letter. The subject needs airing."

I saw the woman who was supposed to be writing me the letter the next afternoon. She told me that her boss, the head of an NEH division, wanted me to call him. "I'll call him at the break," I said. "I hear you're going to write me. What are you going to say?"

"You'll see when you get my letter."

I called her boss. He said, "Some people around here are very upset at what you wrote."

"Is there anything wrong or untrue in what I wrote?"

"That's not it. That's not what they're upset about."

"Do *you* think there's anything wrong or untrue in what I wrote?"

"Of course not. I agree with you. You're more right than you know. But articles like yours can have a chilling effect on applications. If people read that sort of thing, they won't apply, and the fact is that we do manage to get some of those projects through. If people aren't even applying, then even more damage is done."

I asked him if he thought that was the best way to handle the problem—to pretend publicly it didn't exist and to smuggle one or two refugees across the border when the moon was dark. He said it was all he knew how to do and it was better than doing nothing. I said that was how I felt about my editorial. "Well," he said, "You'll be getting a letter on the matter from ______." He named the same woman I'd been told about by the person at NEA.

The letter never came and I never heard anything more about the matter from anyone at NEH. At least not directly. I had an application in process at NEH about that time, one I'd been invited by staff to submit. The announcement deadline passed and I never heard whether the proposal had been funded or rejected, so I called the director of the program, a man I'd never met but with whom I'd talked on the phone a few times. He seemed very embarrassed. "Your project wasn't funded," he said. I expressed some regret, but nothing more: in the world of arts and humanities grant seeking, one expects to fail some or even most of the time; the competition is high and panels can be directed by one or two people with a particular orientation. I've had many grants, but I've filed many more grant applications. Rejection is always disappointing, but the failure of an application to get funding isn't anything extraordinary.

So I was ready to let this one go, perhaps to apply again the following year with a revision of the same proposal that took into consideration the review panel's objections. The director of the program continued talking, and I realized that the panel's objections probably weren't at issue. A revised application wasn't likely to have any greater success than the one that had just been rejected.

"You have to understand," he said. "Sometimes everybody thinks a proposal is terrific, the staff likes it and the panel gives it a very high rating, but then it just disappears upstairs. They don't tell us why those projects disappear, but they do. Not all the decisions are made at this level. Do you hear what I'm saying?"

I said I did and I thanked him for his frankness. "You should try us again sometime," he said. "Reapply."

"Really?"

"Well, you know how these things go."

A friend to whom I recounted the conversation said, "Of course, you dope. What did you think they were going to do up there, thank you for having written those things about them?"

No, of course I hadn't expected thanks, I said, but I rather thought they'd have bent over backwards to be fair to a critic, to prove they really weren't political at heart or vindictive in practice.

"You really *are* a dope," my friend said.

One happy note: largely in response to the kind of criticism quoted in the PBS section of this talk, the Corporation for Public Broadcasting (CPB) has set up the Independent Television Project, a program in which independent filmmakers administer production grants for other independent filmmakers. It's too early to know if this will really end the control of CPB funding by the more powerful stations, but it may very well be a minor breakthrough.

HENRI KORN OF INSTITUT PASTEUR in Paris and Don Faber of the University of Buffalo Medical School have spent much of the past twenty years studying the Mathner cell in carp. The Mathner cell is the nerve that gets them all doing the same thing at the same time when they're frightened. The behavior is called *escape response.* Fish that have a good Mathner cell function survive longer than fish that do not. Other fish have Mathner cells and exhibit the escape response, but for technical reasons Henri and Don prefer the carp version. The carp they use is the one we call goldfish. They have learned a great deal about the way nerves function and communicate and adapt through their studies of that goldfish nerve and its dendrites. But that's not why I'm interested in it.

I'm more interested in the apparent miracle of the fish. There they are in the aquarium, perfectly bounded by the bottom, through which they cannot see; the surface, which they will never transcend; and the four hard transparent sides, through which they can never go. Tap the glass (even though the keeper of the pet shop or the friend whose fish tank it is told you not to) and they all execute that identical escape response on the instant. If they're facing you, suddenly you're seeing their tails; if they're facing left, suddenly they're facing right.

The amazing part isn't that when the stimulus happens they do something; it's that they all do the *same* something, and each fish is acting with absolute and perfect independence of every other fish. The only thing linking them, the water in which they are all suspended, has no apparent function in any of this except as the medium through which the message travels—in this case the reverberation of the tap on the glass. Each fish receives that message and, like a Marine precision drill team, each fish responds to it in exactly the same way.

You may wonder why I'm telling you this, since our concern here is editing reality, not aquatic behavior. I mention the carp and their Mathner cells and the taps on the glass because they are depressingly similar to the forces and agencies that control which of those academic and documentary realities get edited in the first place and which of those edited realities see light of day.

We like to think that we select and execute the projects that are of interest to us in some utterly personal fashion, but in fact our choices are all too often significantly modulated by externals, by taps on the glass.

The participants in this symposium are all scholars and artists who gather information from the world and edit it into something usable by others. They do the editorial alchemy of converting field notes and tapes into books and recordings, or editing miles of raw and—to all eyes but theirs—inchoate footage into films and videotapes. To the results of their editing we have immediate access.

But they're not the only editors of reality. Nor are they the only editors of their own vision of it.

There is, in both academic and media contexts, another class of people entirely who are also central to the process of documenting, editing, and presenting reality. They are never quoted or cited; their names are not attached in significant ways to any of the documents of our concern, and they bear or accept at most minor public responsibility for the success or failure of those objects. Their names are unknown to the general public; often their names are inaccessible even to those whose options they fix or whose work they judge.

They set the terms and conditions under which the scholars and artists and journalists perform. They say, "You will or won't have this grant." They say, "We will or we won't broadcast your film or publish your article or book." They say, "Make these changes and you're in; don't make these changes and you're not."

They're the program editors at PBS. They're the editors of *Harper's* and *American Anthropologist* and the *New York Times* and the CBS "Evening News." They're the executives in private research organizations manipulating data upon which public policy is made. They're panelists and program officers at such agencies as the National Endowment for the Humanities and National Science Foundation.

They are the gatekeepers. Some of those gatekeepers edit our reports of reality directly; they take our vision of the world and they tinker with it so it fits their vision of the world. Other gatekeepers define the context so we edit *ourselves* in ways we otherwise might not. In large measure, these gatekeepers define what kind of work will be done and what kind of work will not be done.

People who are successful at the kinds of work done by participants in this symposium are extremely rational. We may look or act eccentric at times, but it's just a pose, I assure you. Designing, shooting, and editing movies, and formulating, carrying out, and making sense of fieldwork are extremely complex enterprises. Slobs are incapable of such work. Slobs may putter at it, but they can't do it. Being extremely rational, we are, in our work, always trying to get exact answers to three critical questions: *What,* exactly do we want to do? How, exactly, shall we *pay for* it? And what, exactly, shall we *do* with it?

At the very moment we're defining our projects we're looking around for funding and ahead to publication or distribution. We don't hover overlong on projects that don't get funded, nor do we invest much time in projects we know will never be finished or published or distributed. Documentary filmmaking, for example, is extremely expensive and it is physically difficult; I don't know anyone who does it for private or long-delayed consumption. Our editing of reality begins with the definition of subject, it is modulated by our sense of available resources, and the process continues until some publisher or distributor takes it off our hands.

I'm going to be talking mostly about academics and nonfiction filmmakers, but I'd ask you to keep in mind that the other presenters of reality are likewise influenced by the other external editors of reality. Television news, for example, is, like *National Geographic,* picture-driven: the value of a story is usually directly proportional to the amount and quality of film footage accompanying it. The television news editors fear stories without pictures because they believe their audiences won't tolerate mere words. When South Africa and Israel banished film cameras from areas of conflict, the time allotted those subjects on evening news broadcasts shriveled. The